LEARNING RESOURCES CTR/NEW ENGLAND TECH.
GEN   VM341.B53 1986
          Boat and motor facts, fixe

3 0147 0001 2738 4

VM341   S0-EIJ-484

Boat and motor facts, fixes &
tips.

MOTOR FACTS, FIXES & TiPS

1st EDITION

Published by

INTERTEC PUBLISHING CORPORATION
P.O. Box 12901, Overland Park, Kansas 66212

©Copyright 1986 by Intertec Publishing Corp. Printed in
the United States of America.

Cover photograph courtesy of Evinrude Motors.

Library of Congress Catalog Card Number 86-80557

The publisher has exercised reasonable care in compiling the information contained in this manual. The publisher does not guarantee the applications set forth in this manual to the extent that the operation of the equipment and its accessories may be subject to outside influences or factors which cannot be reasonably foreseen. The publisher shall in no way be liable for damages of any description to persons or property, whether incidental or consequential or otherwise related to the use of this manual and in no event shall the liability of the publisher exceed the price paid for this manual.

These Boat and Motor Facts, Fixes & Tips are provided to assist you in obtaining general information concerning the proper use and maintenance of your unit. It is not designed for one specific model. All manufacturers maintain the policy of continual design and manufacturing improvements, which requires that models, specifications and equipment be subject to change without notice. It is for this reason we wish to point out that in the event of conflicting instructions, illustrations or other descriptions, the information furnished by the respective component manufacturer's publications should be followed.

CONTENTS

(By Starting Page Number)

CONTENTS Continued

CONTENTS Continued

CONTENTS Continued

PREFACE

This collection of Boat and Motor Facts, Fixes & Tips was designed to help you understand proper maintenance of your boat, motor and accessories. We've included a variety of information to help you, the veteran as well as less experienced boater, reduce breakdowns, enhance your comfort, increase the value of your boat and generally improve the quality of your boating experiences.

Most of the information in this book will be useful to all, but special sections are included that describe maintenance unique to specific systems that are not used on all boats. As an example, maintenance to the diesel fuel system may only be important if your boat is powered by a diesel engine.

A primary goal of this publication is to impress the importance of **always** thinking and practicing safety while engaged in any activity, including boat maintenance. The boat operator is ultimately responsible for the safety of his passengers, his boat and himself.

We hope you'll find this book an important reference tool immediately and are sure that it will remain a valuable reference source after many successful years of boating.

We wish you many enjoyable and safe years of boating.

The Editors
Technical Publications

THE DEALER

Selecting a dealership is as important as selecting the boat and motor. It will be necessary to buy some parts from an authorized dealer and it may be necessary to find a servicing dealer to perform the more difficult repairs and inspections. In some localities, it might require some extra mileage to find the good dealer who will work with you, but it will be worth it if you must depend heavily on a dealer.

When evaluating a dealership, consider the following points:

1. Is the dealership clean and well-organized?

2. Are the service and parts department areas clean, well-organized and efficient?

3. Are the service and parts department hours convenient for you?

Try to build a good business relationship with the dealership personnel. Note the word BUSINESS here. They are there to make a living just like everyone else. Don't monopolize their time with unnecessary chitchat when there are other customers waiting. When you enter the dealership for parts or service, know as much about the part you need or the problem you are having as you possible can. Insufficient information can make the job more difficult for the partsman or mechanic and may force you to travel home for needed information.

Be just as friendly to the dealership personnel as you expect them to be to you. This friendly attitude may result in some special help in the future.

WARRANTIES

The manufacturer's warranty is designed to cover defects in material and workmanship. This warranty is provided by the manufacturer but many warranty problems can be handled at the dealer level. Since the warranties vary from manufacturer to manufacturer, it is important that warranty on the unit be carefully read and discussed with the dealer.

Normally, warranty does not extend to damage from neglect, accidents, misuse, failure to follow normal or recommended service procedures, failure to use or follow instructions, lack of proper maintenance, normal fair wear and tear, unauthorized repairs or unauthorized modifications to any part that might cause defective performance. The manufacturer does not assume the responsibility for loss of use, loss of time, inconvenience or expenses due to equipment failure.

Be careful to notice that attempts to repair a defect or modify any part may void the manufacturer's warranty. Consider the consequences before making any unauthorized changes.

The boat manufacturer assumes no responsibility or liability for defects in the workmanship or operation of separately warranted products. These products are warranted by the individual manufacturers and a copy of their warranty should be included in the owners packet. In order to obtain repairs or replacement of these items, the individual manufacturers warranty cards must be submitted within ten (10) days of date of purchase.

If service or parts are required, refer to the furnished list of factory authorized service centers. If the list is not available for the particular products, write or call the manufacturer concerned to obtain the location of the nearest authorized service center.

MAINTENANCE FACTS

These maintenance helps contain procedures generally considered usual installation or service and periodic or preventive maintenance. These procedures include cleaning, adjusting and lubricating regularly serviced items. Also, installation of some accessories and trim is included.

MAINTAINING BOAT HULL AND FITTINGS

Almost everything responds in a very positive way to cleaning. The surfaces of the boat hull, deck and fittings should be cleaned often and inspected carefully while cleaning. Inspecting does nothing to change the condition, but the decision to repair a damaged part can be made intelligently only after knowing the extent of the damage. If noticed early most damage is easier and cheaper to repair.

Always thoroughly clean, dry and inspect the boat hull every time the boat is removed from the water. All boat hulls should be coated with a protective covering of wax, oil, paint, etc.

All boats regardless of construction material or type should be cleaned regularly. In addition to the usual positive effects of cleaning, the surfaces can be inspected easily at the same time. Inspecting does nothing to change the condition of the vessel, but the decision to repair a damaged part can only be intelligently made after knowing the extent of the damage.

The frequency of cleaning and the procedure used should be carefully decided in advance of the actual cleaning operation and should not be contingent upon the amount of time remaining. Plan to use sufficient time for cleaning especially before extended periods of boating inactivity.

"Experts" seldom agree about exactly how to clean or what wax to use, but most prefer that hull and all brightwork fittings be completely cleaned and dried whenever possible. This doesn't mean scrubbing all metal daily, but does mean that boats should be thoroughly cleaned and dried each time they are removed from the water. This is frequent cleaning for many trailered boats, but it is important to clean boats that remain in the water too. Boats operating in salt water or heavily polluted waters are especially susceptible to major permanent damage if not frequently cleaned.

When boats made of fiberglass first appeared on the market, it was believed to be the material that would put an end to periodic maintenance work. Even though fiberglass will not deteriorate like wood, nor will it rust or corrode like a steel or aluminum boat hull, periodic inspection and maintenance must be performed to keep the hull exterior looking like new.

HULL & DECK

Coatings of weeds, barnacles, grassy slime, salt or dirt and stains from exhaust, rust or tarnish detract from the appearance and may affect performance measurably. The hull bottom should be as smooth and clean as possible for maximum fuel efficiency and performance. Special finishes may require special cleaners or waxes, but it is best if cleaning occurs before a noticeable buildup occurs on the hull.

Hull surfaces are usually painted, anodized or gel coated. All hull surfaces should be kept clean, but most require some form of special attention.

Antifouling bottom paints should never be waxed, but should always be kept clean. Choose to use antifouling paint very carefully, then use extreme caution when selecting the specific type of paint, because some may increase corrosion of the motor and/or lower unit and some may even be a health hazard. Most antifouling paints contain a material that dissolves or leaches from the paint. The erosion of the material is sometimes even faster when removed from the water than when submerged. Always consult sources that are knowledgeable about your boat, motor and the water in which it is used for determining what type of antifouling paint to use, proper application methods, correct maintenance procedures and ways of recognizing when paint should be applied again.

Surfaces painted with any usual types of paint (not antifouling bottom paint) should be kept clean and waxed. Paint formulated for underwater use may be different than paints used for topside finishing. Cleaning can usually be accomplished using a mild nonabrasive detergent. Stains or severely weathered painted surfaces can sometimes be bleached or removed using a variety of cleaning agents including lacquer thinner, abrasive cleansers and fine sand paper, but use of any of these should be limited because damage may result which would require repainting. Use a good quality wax specified for marine application. **Automotive waxes should not be used.** Some marine wax can be applied to a damp hull, but some types require that the hull be completely dry. Be sure to use wax as directed by the manufacturer.

The anodized surface of aluminum boats should not be scratched or otherwise damaged by cleaning. The dull, often colored, surface coat of most aluminum used on boat hulls, fittings, spars or accessories is a very thin protective anodized layer that slows damage caused by oxidation. Abrasive cleansers, polishes, brushes or anything else that rubs away this protective layer will expose unprotected base metal that will deteriorate much faster. Once the protective outer anodized surface of aluminum is removed it is important to protect the remaining metal at all times with paint or wax. Aluminum can be polished using fine steel wool and soap; however, it is important to apply paint or wax frequently to prevent further corrosion.

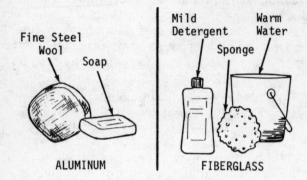

ALUMINUM   FIBERGLASS

Gel coated surfaces of fiberglass boats should be carefully washed with mild detergent, warm water and soft bristled brushes or a sponge. Do not use abrasive cleansers, stiff brushes, metal wool pads or any other cleaning medium that would scratch the gel coat surface. Use strong cleaning solvents very cautiously, making sure the types used will not damage the fiberglass or gel coat. Never permit any cleaning solution, including soap, to dry on the surface. Wash area carefully, rinse with fresh water, then dry with soft cloth or chamois. Wax gel coat surfaces with a good quality marine wax. **Automotive waxes should not be used.** Some marine wax can be applied to a damp hull, but some types require that hull be completely dry while applying. Be sure to use wax as directed by the manufacturer.

HELPFUL HINT

Salt water stains can often be prevented by soaking shoes or clothes in a solution of 1 part vinegar and 2 parts fresh water. Allow shoes and clothes to dry slowly in the sun. The smell should soon evaporate and leather shoes may be softened with saddle soap.

Inflatable boats may become coated with a marine growth that is difficult to remove except with a strong solution of liquid bleach and fresh water. The bleach will not only kill the growth, but will loosen its grip so that it can be more easily removed from the bottom fabric. A coating of marine wax may slow future growth.

FITTINGS & TRIM

There are four types of metal commonly used to manufacture brightwork fittings for boats: Stainless steel, Bronze, Chrome plate and Aluminum. Each type of metal requires special care, but all must be cleaned frequently. Moisture and air, two things commonly found around boats, are required for metal fittings to oxidize. These metals are, however, much more susceptible to chemical damage when a pollutant is also present. Salt air, dirt and even some caustic cleaning solutions help oxidation begin and daily cleaning will slow the process measurably. Washing with a mild soap and water followed by a thorough rinse with fresh water is suggested after each cruise or at least once each week. Use a sponge, cloth or soft brush to clean salt, dirt, etc., especially from crevices and joints of fittings. Salt is particularly damaging to aluminum especially if the metal isn't painted, anodized or otherwise protected.

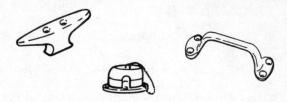

Stainless steel is supposedly corrosion-resistant, but the quality used for boat fittings varies greatly. Even the best will become dull and tarnished if neglected and poorer quality will pit and develop surface corrosion quickly. Rust around a stainless steel fitting may be caused by metal imbedded by the tools used to machine the part, steel screws used to mount the fitting or by impurities in the stainless steel itself. Special cleaning material, which is a cotton wadding impregnated with a chemical solution, can be used for usual cleaning and polishing of stainless steel. The cotton material should be used only until all surfaces turn very dark, then discarded. The chemical from the cotton cleaning material should leave a hazy film on the stainless steel fixture. Polish the fixture with a soft clean cloth after the cleaner has been allowed to dry for a few minutes. A metal polish containing abrasive, available from marine and auto service stores, may be necessary if surfaces are severely oxidized. After cleaning and polishing, use paint thinner or similar solvent to remove cleaning residue, then clean the fixture completely with water and dry with a soft cloth. Regardless of any claims by the manufacturer of the cleaner, apply a separate coat of liquid wax that is formulated to fight rust to all cleaned and polished stainess steel surfaces. An old sweat sock makes a great buffer when used like a glove to polish fixtures.

Chrome plated parts are usually cleaned easily using a mild soap and water. Rinse soap off using fresh water, then dry using a chamois or soft absorbent cloth. If chrome plating doesn't shine after cleaning, then carefully determine the extent and cause of damage to surface before continuing. Plating may be stained or painted in which case a suitable solvent may be used to remove the offending coating. Some chrome plated parts may be coated with a clear protective finish that will, like paint, dull with age. Any abrasive should be used very cautiously on chrome plated surfaces and is not often recommended. Pitted surfaces in chrome plating is repaired only by installing a new similar part. Frequent cleaning and coating with a penetrating lubricant may arrest further damage by protecting metal from further oxidation and pitting. All chrome plating can be protected by coating with WD-40, LPS-1, CRC or similar moisture displacing lubricant. Apply only a light film, but be sure that lubricant enters any cracks, joints or pits. Wipe off any excess that would hold dirt. Liquid wax, a light coat of clear lacquer or other protective coating may also be used to help protect especially difficult to reach and/or clean parts.

Bronze fittings and trim will quickly tarnish and oxidize if not coated with a protective finish. The familiar dark gray to green film usually does little to damage the metal, but may detract from the overall appearance of the boat. The stain may also continue down over painted or gel coated surfaces. Begin cleaning using a strong detergent and special bronze wool pads. Polish the bronze part using a commercial product or with a solution of salt and vinegar. After metal is cleaned and bright, rinse with fresh water and dry carefully making sure that your skin doesn't touch the part at any time. The usual coating for bronze is clear lacquer or similar clear paint spray. If the paint is worn away or nicked, all of the clear coating must be removed before recoating. Application of moisture-displacing lubricants (WD-40, LPS-1, CRC or similar) can be successfully used to prevent bronze from tarnishing, but must be done frequently. Other coatings including clear teak oil have also been used with varying degrees of success.

CANVAS AND VINYL COVERS AND TOPS

Covers and folding tops should be cleaned often to prevent stains and damage. Check attached labels or instructions provided by manufacturer for approved cleaning solutions and methods. Most materials can be cleaned with a **mild** liquid detergent, but abrasive detergents and harsh cleaning solvents will probably cause damage. Be sure that all soap is rinsed from material after cleaning. Cover or top should be cleaned before storing.

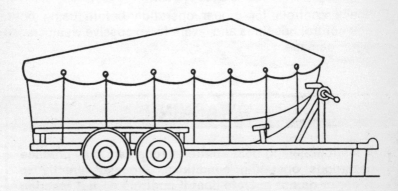

Dry the covers and tops completely before storing. Mold or mildew can begin very quickly to damage material if stored even for a short time while still damp. Mold and mildew are very difficult to remove from all types of fabric. Shrinkage will be reduced if covers and tops are installed while drying.

Vinyl is easily damaged by attempting to stretch, fold or unfold while cold. All types of material may shrink if folded or stored for an extended time. If possible, all tops and fitted covers should be installed during storage.

Color may fade from fabrics after extended exposure to sunlight. Blocking exposure to sun by covering will reduce fading. Be careful that all covers used will allow air to circulate and do not hold moisture that could cause mold, mildew and rotting.

BOAT INTERIOR

The interior of the boat includes, the cabin, galley, head and bunks as well as the seats, storage compartments, windshield, portholes, deck and bilge. A major concern regarding this area of any boat is eliminating all chances of fire. Use flammable solvent only while boat is removed from the water and with immediate access to sufficient fire fighting equipment. Extra engine fuel, flammable cleaning solvent, paint, etc., should never be stored onboard.

CONTROLS

Check controls for proper operation before using boat. Check control housings and levers for excessive wear, cracks or other damage.

⚠WARNING

A malfunctioning boat control mechanism may produce hazardous operating conditions. Proceed directly to shore or do not operate boat if controls do not function properly.

On models with pump-driven power steering or hydraulic steering, inspect all lines and hoses for damage. Check tightness of all fittings and clamps regularly and maintain correct fluid level. Pump drive belt should be inspected for tension, wear and damage. Install new belt if damaged; adjust belt tension if loose. Contact your dealer for servicing help and for proper operating fluid and lubricants.

Cables are used to link the operator with the various parts providing control of most boat operations. These vital links wear very little and because they seldom cause trouble, cables are usually ignored.

Obviously any control malfunction calls for immediate inspection of the cables affecting that operation, but each control system should be routinely checked for smooth operation with constant, even resistance to movement. If operation is jerky or if controls stick at certain spots, the cables should be thoroughly inspected immediately.

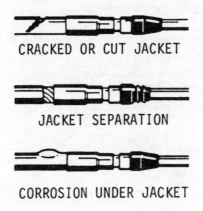

CRACKED OR CUT JACKET

JACKET SEPARATION

CORROSION UNDER JACKET

Many problems can be detected visually. First, check for corrosion of end fittings or connection parts. Salt or other deposits should be removed from end connecting parts regularly, before much buildup is noticed. Coat ends with an appropriate oil or marine grease to reduce buildup. Rust, corrosion or other damage to the controlling parts is usually repaired by installing new parts, so reducing damage by frequent cleaning and lubrication will extend useful life of these parts.

Check for signs of cable abrasion which may wear through. Relocate cable if necessary to prevent premature failure. Abrasion of cable at a pulley indicates that pulley isn't turning and should be repaired or that cable is not properly located on the pulley.

Check the plastic cable jacket for cracks or cuts which will permit moisture to enter the housing and rust or corrode the cable. A common location for failure to occur is where the jacket is joined to the metal end fittings. A swelling of the plastic jacket is an indication of corrosion inside the jacket or a possible heat source too close to the plastic covering. Check swelled areas closely and install a new cable if any sticking is indicated.

Any damage to the cable or housing is reason to install a new assembly. Taping the plastic jacket and lubricating the cable inside the housing are seldom successful repairs, but usually only mask the damage. Serious failure can result from the false and dangerous sense of security resulting from masking the evidence of damage.

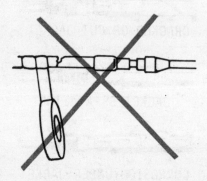

CORROSION

Corrosion is the activity during which refined metals change back to their natural state. Corrosion can be destruction by chemical action or the electrochemical reaction to a metal's environment. Common forms are recognized by the rusting of iron and the gray/white corrosion of aluminum.

Movement of electrons through a conductor from a nonstable metal to a metal that is more stable removes small pieces of the material from the least stable (anode). Common metals used around boats beginning at the most anodic are magnesium, aluminum, maganese, zinc, chromium, iron, nickel, tin, lead, copper and silver. The process can be accelerated by improving the electrolyte (conductor), raising the temperature and causing electrical current to flow between the metals.

Above the waterline the conductor is primarily warm humid air with occasional moist spray and the result is oxidation of the metal parts. The major contributors to the corrosion process are the heat and oxygen aided by the moist environment. Protection above the waterline is provided by separating metals with different electromotive force (emf) ratings, keeping similar metals together and sealing metal surfaces to prevent contact with the conductor. Waxing and painting parts are examples of sealing the metal to help prevent oxidation. Attaching an aluminum fitting with brass screws is an example of not separating dissimilar metals and will surely result in early corrosion damage to the aluminum.

Below the waterline, the conductor is water. The quality of the water as an eletrolyte will affect the speed at which corrosion damage occurs. Salt water is a much better electrolyte than most fresh water, therefore corrosion damage will occur more quickly in the salt water environment. Boats are generally used during warm weather and are often heated by the sun. The higher temperature will contribute to faster corrosion. Of course, the same methods of protecting metal parts above the waterline are applicable; but the environment (water) is more hostile. Simple coatings of wax or paint are easily penetrated and will not seal the surfaces for very long. Separating metals with different emf ratings is seldom possible, because natural ore, iron or steel anchors, car bodies, etc., are often in the water (that is the conductor fluid) with the propeller and drive lower unit. Movement of electrical current through the water will greatly accelerate the speed of corrosion damage. This electrical current is often stray current leakage from the battery, a motor or the charging system that is not noticed and doesn't affect the satisfactory operation of the systems. Electrical current passing from one metal part through the water to another is actually the movement of electrons from one part to another. This movement of electrons will cause small pieces of material to be removed from the negatively charged piece as the electrons flow through the conductor toward the metal which has the positive charge. Sacrificial metals can be installed that will use these principles to help protect other parts from corrosion. Follow instructions provided by the manufacturer, but sacrificial metal is usually magnesium or zinc located below the water line on the lower part of the transom and is connected to the electrical system negative ground. The sacrificial metal should not be too large or protection may be reversed. The electrical connection between the sacrificial metal and the system ground must be in very good condition. Check the condition of the sacrificial metal regularly, because it will erode away if it is operating properly and should be replaced before it is completely eroded.

HELPFUL HINT

Quick setting epoxy can be used for a variety of repairs. The epoxy is available both as a semi-solid putty and in liquid form. Each type has practical application for emergency repair, can be stored for long periods and is easy to use. Slow curing epoxy is usually not fast enough for emergency repairs.

The engine cooling passages and connecting tubing are subjected to corrosion which can destroy engine parts including major components such as cylinder block and cylinder head. To reduce damage, each metal part, including hose clamps should be connected electrically. Parts that are bolted together are usually common electrically, but it will be necessary to connect remote or insulated metal parts to the engine block and cylinder head using wire. Multistrand copper wire is suggested. Connecting the various metal parts with wire will equalize the electrical potential of each part and is called BONDING. Special plugs made of sacrificial metal (usually zinc or magensium) are sometimes installed in the cooling system. If used, be sure sacrificial metal plugs are bonded to the remainder of the metal parts of the cooling system.

MAINTAINING CABINS, GALLEY BUNKS AND HEAD

TEAK

Teak may be one of many varities and the color varies from a wide grained, golden color to close grained, red color when clean. Dry wood will be grayish in color, oxidize rapidly and stain easily. Teak should be kept clean and properly oiled at all times. Many special cleansers, oil and sealing products are available and should be used as explained by the manufacturers. Oils/sealers should be applied evenly to clean wood. Oil will build up if too much is applied or if old oil is not removed first. Special care products are also available for maintenance between major cleaning and sealing operations as well as for changing the color of the wood.

Special products for cleaning, oiling and protecting, teak finishes should not harm adjacent surfaces including seam compounds. Most manufacturers of cleansers and sealers recommend removing their products from all surfaces except the wood. However, some people suggest that some teak oil can be used to protect bronze from corrosion.

VARNISH

Stir varnish only if absolutely necessary, such as after adding thinner. If stirring is required, be very careful, stir gently, use a wide paddle; then let varnish stand for at least one hour before using. Air bubbles caused by stirring should all be gone before attempting to apply varnish with a brush. It will be almost impossible to apply a smooth finish coat if varnish contains air bubbles caused by vigorous shaking or stirring.

WALLS AND DECKS

Walls, decks and other surfaces may be any of several finishes or textures. Strong detergents and abrasive cleansers are not recommended. Most surfaces will clean with a soft cloth which has been dampened with a mild liquid detergent mixed with warm water. Strong cleaning solvents such as acetone, lacquer thinner and some chemical cleansers may be required for removing oil, grease stains or scuff marks. Use these strong solvents very cautiously because of fire hazard and possible damage to paint, fiberglass or other surfaces. Rewash surfaces cleaned with strong solvents with mild soap, then rinse completely. Cleaning, even with a mild soap, will remove wax protection from surface. All surfaces should be as dry as possible when finished cleaning. Apply suitable wax protection to appropriate surfaces after cleaned surface is dry.

Contact boat manufacturer or local servicing marina if coating deck surfaces with nonskid material. Some coatings require special application procedures and nonskid material may damage deck or protective coating.

GALLEY

Allow surfaces heated by cooking to cool, then clean with hot soapy water. Use a damp cloth to clean chrome surfaces. Grease splatters, which may bake onto surfaces, should be wiped off before they have time to harden. Use a toothpick to clean clogged burner ports. Clean oven with commercial cleaner as necessary.

⚠CAUTION

DO NOT apply oven cleaner to any aluminum tubing, any aluminum or painted surface, the thermostat sensing bulb or any electrical component.

If equipped with a range hood, first remove the light cover and wash it with a mild detergent and water. Remove the filter and clean with hot soapy water until grease is dissolved. Rinse filter with clean water, then allow to dry. Clean grease from housing, fan and motor surfaces, then reinstall filter with arrows pointing in toward housing. A good glass cleaner can be used to clean and polish chrome trim.

Food and ice should not be left in refrigerator. Remove everything from inside refrigerator and clean interior with warm water and liquid dish soap. Rinse, then wipe dry with a soft cloth. DO NOT use abrasive cleaning material because it will scratch interior surfaces. Turn controls OFF during extended periods of nonuse. Door should be blocked open to permit air circulation whenever refrigerator is turned off.

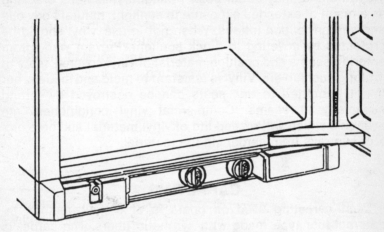

POTABLE WATER SYSTEM

The potable water system should be completely sanitized upon delivery (before its first use), after any long period of nonuse and after any suspected contamination. There are various commercial solutions available to assist you in sanitizing the system or you can use the one which follows:

Prepare a chlorine solution using one gallon of water and ¼-cup of household bleach (5% sodium hypochlorite solution). With water tank empty, pour one gallon of solution into tank for each 15 gallons of tank capacity. Complete filling of tank with fresh water. Open faucets to release air. Pressurize system with pump until water flows, then turn off pump and faucets. Allow to stand for three hours. Drain and flush with potable fresh water.

To remove excessive chlorine taste or odor which may remain, prepare a solution of one quart vinegar to five gallons of water and allow solution to agitate in water tank by vehicle motion (several days if possible). Drain tank and again flush with potable fresh water.

SEATS

Vinyl seat coverings and trim can usually be wiped clean with a moist cloth or sponge. A mild liquid detergent mixed with water or a cleanser designed for cleaning vinyl material may be necessary for cleaning seats that are espically dirty. Some solvents and most abrasive cleansers may harm vinyl. Vinyl material may suffer color fading, dryness and cracking as a result of extended exposure to sunlight, natural body oils and sun protection lotions. When not in use, vinyl should be protected by covering to block sunlight. Prevent water from entering seams and cushion material/of vinyl covered seats to prolong cushion life. Vinyl is resistant to mold and mildew, but if not permitted to dry, seats can be destroyed by rotting especially at seams. Commercial vinyl conditioners are available which will extend life of vinyl material and help protect sun rays from hardening the material.

CARPETING

Most carpeting used on boats is of the all-weather, indoor/outdoor type made with synthetic fibers. The carpet is usually resistant to water and sun damage, but extended exposure to either will probably damage the carpet.

Carpeting should not be allowed to remain wet for very long. Mildew and mold may cause discoloration and odor that can only be removed by installing new carpeting. Wet carpeting can also cause deck surfaces (particularly wood decking) to rot if carpet is permitted to remain wet too long. Trailered or dry docked boats can usually be tilted and drain plugs can be removed to permit water to drain from carpet and closed compartments. It may be necessary to use a special vacuum cleaner or carpet cleaner to remove water from carpets in enclosed areas or from cabins below deck.

⚠WARNING

If a vacuum cleaner is used, be sure to use one that can safely remove water without danger of electrical shock to operator. All electrical equipment should be properly grounded as directed by the manufacturer for safe operation.

Direct sunlight will damage most carpeting to some extent. Carpeting close to light colored or polished, reflective surfaces will often burn and be discolored before surrounding carpeting. To reduce damage caused by exposure to sun, cover with light blocking cover when boat is not in use. Covering during storage can also protect from water damage, if cover prevents entrance of water and is properly vented. Do not trap moisture inside by sealing cover. If exposed to accumulation of snow, be sure that cover does not sag and attempt to hold snow and water.

Cleaning

The carpet should be cleaned frequently. Salt, food, mud, etc., will reduce the life of carpeting. Embedded dirt can be removed by scrubbing with a mild soap and fresh water. Be sure to rinse thoroughly using plenty of fresh water, then use appropriate methods to be sure that carpet is allowed to dry. Special carpet cleaning machines are available for rent that will clean carpet easily, but be sure the machine is properly grounded and used correctly to prevent electrical shock.

Installing

Carpet is easier to maintain and replace if not fastened down at all, but it must not be a hazard that can cause people to trip. Often glue is used to attach carpet to the complete deck surface, but other methods such as double-sided tape and "Velcro" strips may also be considered. Regardless of method used to attach carpet, it is important that seams, wrinkles and edges will not trip passengers or crew, especially during an emergency.

All of the old carpet should be removed and the surface covered by the carpet should be smooth, clean and dry. It may be necessary to ask your boat dealer for appropriate method of removing old glue or tape.

⚠WARNING

Sanders and some chemical removers may damage fiberglass and painted surfaces. Sanding dust and some solvents used to remove glue may cause a fire hazard. Also, respiratory injury can result from breathing sanding dust or solvent fumes. Be sure that area is adequately ventilated, and safe from spark or ignition source. Use correct mask to prevent inhaling dust.

Glue can be used to stick the carpet firmly in place over the complete surface, but consult your boat dealer and carpet manufacturer for approved adhesive that will not damage either the deck or the new carpet.

Double-sided tape or "Velcro" is especially useful where carpet must be removed for access or where easy removal is advantageous.

⚠️DANGER

Do not cover any hatch or access in such a way that entrance is blocked. If hatch has handle or lift ring, remove carpet covering the handle. Carpet should be marked to identify hatches that may need to be found and opened during any emergency.

GLASS

All windshields, light covers, hatch covers, etc., on boats should use only approved safety glass or a synthetic material such as "Plexiglass" or "Lexan". Each of the approved materials can be scratched if rubbed with an abrasive cleanser, but some materials (such as "Plexiglass") are more easily scratched than others.

Use only a mild liquid soap or a good quality cleanser approved for use on the specific material for cleaning. Scratches can be removed from some synthetic materials using special polishers. Check with dealer for selecting appropriate cleaning or polishing material.

SERVICING ACCESSORIES

BOAT WIRING

Standards have been established by the National Marine Manufacturers Association suggesting the colors of wire used for low voltage (less than 50 volts) direct current (dc) electrical circuits aboard boats. Other colors and wire with contrasting stripe of trace are also used by many manufacturers to indicate other important circuits. Manufacturers often provide specific wiring diagrams to assist connection and to help locate trouble. The following NMMA suggested color code may be helpful if specific diagram is not available.

INSULATION COLOR	USE OR LOCATION
Black	Ground, Negative main power.
Brown	Generator armature to voltage regulator. Alternator charge light. Wire from generator terminal or alternator auxiliary terminal to the charge light and voltage regulator. Pump circuits. Wire from fuses or switches to pumps.
Dark Blue	Cabin and instrument lights. Wire from fuses or switches to lights.
Dark Gray	Navigation lights. Wire from fuses or switches to the lights. Tachometer sender to instrument (gage) wire.
Dark Green	Insulated bonding wires. Some bonding wires may be uninsulated.
Light Blue	Oil pressure sender to instrument (gage) wire.
Orange	Accessory common feed. Wire from ammeter to alternator or generator output and accessory fuses or switches. Wire from the distribution panel to accessory switch terminal.

Pink	Fuel gage. Wire from sender to instrument (gage).
Purple	Ignition and instrument feed. Wire from ignition switch to ignition system coil(s) and electrical instruments.
Red	Positive, main power feed wires.
Red with Purple Stripe	Positive, power feed wires with circuit protection (fusible link).
Tan	Coolant temperature. Wire from temperature sender to instrument (gage).
Yellow	Generator or alternator field. Wire from generator field terminal of the voltage regulator. Bilge blower circuit. Wire from fuse or switch to the bilge blower.
Yellow with Red Stripe	Starting circuit. Wire from starting switch to starter control solenoid.

⚠CAUTION

Be extremely careful to prevent electrical shorts and resulting damage during any testing, modification or service to the electrical system wiring. Suggested or published wiring diagrams and procedures must be used very cautiously because production changes, modifications, damage or errors may cause electricity to pass through wires and components in ways different than expected. Electrical misjudgements or errors will often result in immediate destruction of components.

BOAT EMERGENCY EQUIPMENT

- ☐ Flashlight (extra fresh batteries)
- ☐ Matches
- ☐ Assortment of hand tools
- ☐ Spare fuses & light bulbs
- ☐ Spare propeller, shear pin, cotter pin, etc.
- ☐ Extra set of spark plugs & wrench
- ☐ First Aid Kit
  - ☐ Adhesive bandages (assorted sizes)
  - ☐ Adhesive tape
  - ☐ Antacid
  - ☐ Anti-bacterial ointment, spray, liquid
  - ☐ Antiseptic soap
  - ☐ Aspirin or equivalent
  - ☐ Bandages (assorted size gauze pads)
  - ☐ Burn cream & sunburn medicine
  - ☐ Elastic bandages
  - ☐ Eye wash
  - ☐ Hot water bottle
  - ☐ Motion sickness medicine
  - ☐ Snake bite kit
  - ☐ Thermometer
  - ☐ _____
  - ☐ _____
- ☐ Extra oil (engine, transmission, outboard motor, etc.)
- ☐ _____
- ☐ _____
- ☐ _____
- ☐ _____

NOTE

Stow emergency equipment so that each item can be quickly and easily located. Some items can be moved from one location to another depending upon need, other items may be unique to the boat, the trailer or the tow vehicle, but first aid kits should always be located at the camp, in the tow vehicle and in the boat.

TRAILERING EMERGENCY EQUIPMENT

- ☐ Lug wrench
- ☐ Small jack & boards for blocking
- ☐ Spare wheel & tire (check air pressure before leaving)
- ☐ Tire pump & tire pressure gage
- ☐ Road flares & reflectors
- ☐ Spare lightbulbs
- ☐ Wheel chocks
- ☐ _____
- ☐ _____
- ☐ _____
- ☐ _____

HELPFUL HINT

Locking pliers should not be used in place of proper fitting standard wrenches because the fasteners are almost always destroyed by their use. However, high quality locking pliers are often a valuable aid for emergency clamping, gripping, pulling, pushing or turning. Inexpensive tools of any kind are usually a bad investment and often a safety hazard that won't even work as planned. Locking pliers such as the "Vise Grip" brand are made in several sizes and a selection of two or three different sizes should be sufficient for most emergency repairs.

HELPFUL HINT

A small powerful magnet is often helpful for retrieving tools, bolts, nuts, washers, etc., that are dropped in engine compartment, bilge or similar inaccessible area. A magnetic retrieval tool with a handle is available from most suppliers of tools for automotive and marine repair.

HELPFUL HINT

A hand drill is often easier and safer than a similar power tool. Aluminum, wood and fiberglass can be easily drilled with a hand drill and a small number of holes can be drilled easily without using an extension cord. The hand drill is best if equipped with a ¼ inch chuck; however, large or irregular shaped holes can be cut by drilling a series of small holes that just touch or almost touch. Mark the exact desired size and shape, then scribe a similar line inside the desired mark equal to ½ the diameter of the drill bit being used. Center punch around the inner mark at intervals slightly further apart than the drill bit diameter. Use a file or scraper to clean up rough edge created by the small connected holes.

LUBRICATING HARD-TO-REACH SPOTS

Many lubricating products are now packaged in a pressurized can with a nozzle to spray the lubricant over a large area. Some of these products also have a nozzle that can be adjusted to direct a stream of the lubricant to a specific area and other products include a small plastic tube which can be used to apply lubricant to an even smaller spot. The ones that will spray in any position have a balloon inside the can. Usually, one of these products and the appropriate nozzle can be used effectively. However, it is sometimes desirable to drip a fluid, usually a lubricant, that isn't in a pressurized can onto an almost inaccessible spot. A wire can be used to direct the oil to a specific location in two different ways. One method is to dip the end of a wire into the oil, then move the end of the wire quickly to the spot where the lubricant is needed. Sometimes the engine oil dipstick can be used in this way to oil something. Another method is to direct the wire down to the spot or hole where oil is desired. Drip oil onto the wire near the top and it will run down the wire to the bottom.

⚠CAUTION

Be extremely careful while lubricating cables and always use heavy leather gloves when servicing cables to prevent painful personal injury.

PEDESTAL STEERING

The steering pedestal system should be maintained to ensure proper control. All systems are not alike, but the following procedures will be helpful for many models.

It is necessary to remove the compass and its cylinder before servicing parts at the top of the pedestal. Tape can be located across joint of compass and cylinder and across joint between cylinder and pedestal to help align these parts when assembling. Cut through the tape at the joints of the parts before removing.

Squeeze Teflon #827 or equivalent lubricant into holes in tops of bearing housings to lubricate the needle bearings inside pedestal bowl. Turn the wheel while lubricating to make sure that entire bearing is serviced. Do not let bearings run dry. Normal interval is to grease pedestal bearings once each year; however, on extended voyages the system should be inspected each day and lubricated each week. It is suggested that entire steering system be inspected and lubricated within one week of a planned cruise to avoid problems. Lubricate the chain with SAE 30 oil. Grease will not penetrate the chain links.

Inspect and lightly oil the steering cables once each year. A suggested method is to squirt about 5 facial tissues with SAE 30 oil, then wipe the oiled tissues along full length of cables. This method lubricates the cable and identifies broken strands.

If tissue catches on broken wire indicating damage to the cable, install new steering cable immediately. Steering cables should be removed and replaced with new cable after five years use. The old, but serviceable cable should be carried on board as an emergency spare.

Lock the wheel in position using the pedestal brake or by tying off the wheel, then check cable tension. The quadrant or drive wheel should not be movable with wheel tied off or wheel locked with the brake. Sensitivity will be reduced and wear may increase if cable tension is too tight.

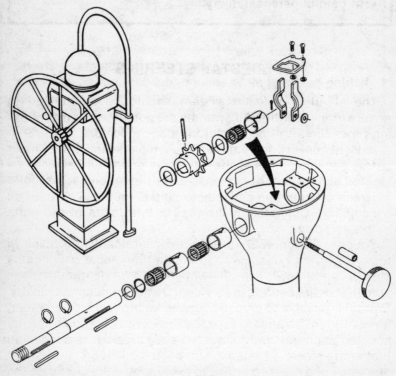

All boats must have an emergency tiller or equivalent and all on board must be familiar with its location and operation. Emergency tiller drill should be conducted regularly, as should the man overboard drill. One person should be assigned the job of maintaining, inspecting and servicing the steering system, but all should be familiar with emergency procedures. Any time anyone notices a strange noise or unusual reaction relating to the steering system, find the cause immediately. Check all screws, nuts, bolts, clevis pins, cotter pins, cables, rods, bearings, etc., for any perceptible looseness. Any distortion, bending, creaking, giving or other indication of failure should be corrected immediately.

The steering wheel should be tied off or should have brake locked all the time that boat is left unattended. Do Not let the steering system freewheel, because uncontrolled movement can damage components.

HELPFUL HINT

Small flecks of rust or light surface corrosion can be removed from control panels, instruments, screws, fishing gear and other small or delicate surfaces using a lead pencil. Rub the spot with the graphite lead to remove the rust and cover the affected area with a light protective coat of graphite. A light coat of clear fingernail polish or paint can be applied to the affected area for a more durable protective coat if desired.

RACK AND PINION STEERING

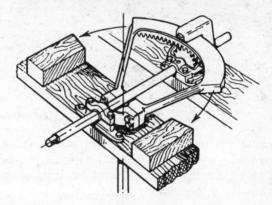

Steering may be controlled by various types of rack and pinion controls. Shaft bearings and gear teeth should be lubricated often. Lubricated parts should never be allowed to operate without a coating of appropriate grease or oil. Check specific requirements for each unit. Steering universal joints should be greased and enclosed in approved boot. Inspect steering daily to be sure that steering operates properly. Lost motion caused by wear or improper adjustment should be repaired or adjusted if excessive.

WORM STEERING

Rudder control may utilize a worm type steering system. Refer to specific manufacturer's service data if possible. Bushings should be lubricated daily with SAE 30 oil. The worm assembly and the steering pivots should be lubricated with Water Pump grease. Check for loose attachment. Misalignment caused by looseness will cause binding. Threads of the traversing nut are often replaceable by specialized repair centers.

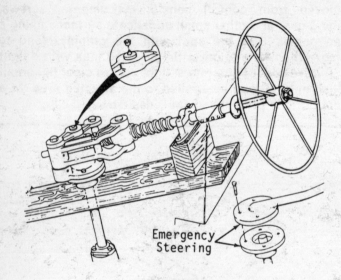

Emergency Steering

BATTERY

Battery current may be used to operate clocks or other equipment which will continue to drain the battery even during extended storage if the battery is not disconnected or removed. Disconnecting the battery ground will stop further drain, but removal is suggested especially if extended storage is in a cold area. The battery fluid can freeze solid at +20°F and freezing will permanently damage the battery.

Checking Condition

First, check visually for external damage such as cracks or holes in the case, eroded terminals or excessive corrosion around terminals. Also check condition of battery cables and cable terminals.

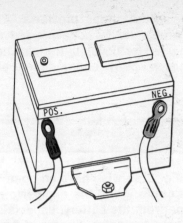

⚠CAUTION

Corroded cables or terminals that result in an open circuit can permanently damage the alternator.

⚠DANGER

Acid from the battery will cause injury upon contact with skin, especially around eyes. Rinse area thoroughly with clean water and consult a doctor immediately. Always wear safety glasses when working near batteries.

If possible, check to be sure that each cell is filled with correct amount of fluid. Fill with distilled water to correct level if fluid is low. Some batteries have individual caps for each cell, other batteries have caps joined together, but each cell is individual and must be filled separately. Some batteries are sealed and cannot be filled, but fluid should not be permitted to escape either. Low fluid level may be caused by tipping battery over, cracking the case, overcharging or overheating.

Each cell of the battery should provide approximately 2 volts Direct Current. Three cells are connected to make a 6 volt battery, six cells are used for 12 volt batteries. The specific gravity of the fluid in a properly charged cell should be about 1.210-1.300.

⚠DANGER

NEVER smoke or otherwise have an open flame near the battery which could ignite the explosive gas. Hydrogen gas will escape from the battery, especially while charging, and is highly explosive. Sparks at battery terminals are often the cause of battery explosions. Injury is possible from the explosion and from exposure to the acid.

Battery condition can be checked by using a hydrometer to check the specific gravity of each cell if a sufficient amount of fluid can be withdrawn. Another method of checking condition is to fully charge the battery, then connect a load tester and voltmeter across the battery terminals. Apply a load sufficient to obtain 300 amperes for 15 seconds to remove the surface charge, let the battery recover for 15 seconds, then apply the proper Test Load and check voltage. The proper Test Load is ½ the cranking performance rating of the battery being checked. Check the voltage after applying the Test Load for 15 seconds. Consult the following chart for suggested minimum voltages at specific ambient air temperatures.

Minimum Voltage	Temperature Degrees F.	Degrees C.
9.6	70	21
9.5	60	16
9.4	50	10
9.3	40	4
9.1	30	− 1
8.9	20	− 7
8.7	10	− 12
8.5	0	− 18

⚠CAUTION

Do not attempt to charge a frozen battery. Thaw the battery before attempting to charge. A discharged battery may freeze solid at 20°F (–7°C) and can be permanently damaged.

NOTE

Some batteries have a built-in hydrometer to help diagnose battery trouble. Most are similar to the Delco battery "eye" shown. The green dot indicates at least 65% charge. If the dot is black, the cell is less than 65% charged. If the dot is clear or light yellow, the electrolyte level is below the level of the hydrometer. Please notice that the battery may only include one built-in hydrometer and each checks only one of the 3 or 6 cells. A good battery will discharge all cells almost evenly, but the failure of a cell not being checked will probably not be indicated.

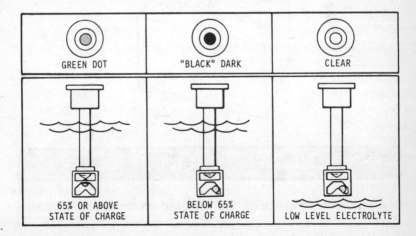

GREEN DOT	"BLACK" DARK	CLEAR
65% OR ABOVE STATE OF CHARGE	BELOW 65% STATE OF CHARGE	LOW LEVEL ELECTROLYTE

⚠CAUTION

Electrical components may be instantly damaged by connecting battery with terminals reversed. Red is often used to indicate the positive (+) terminal connections and black (sometimes blue) is used to indicate negative (−) terminal connections. The battery will be marked "POSITIVE", "POS" or "+" and "NEGATIVE", "NEG" or "−" to indicate polarity of terminals. Be especially careful when attaching battery charger or jumper cables.

If necessary to attach jumper cables, be sure to attach the RED cable to the positive terminal of both batteries. The black cable should be attached to the Negative terminal or connector. Be careful not to cause an electrical spark near the battery when making the final connection.

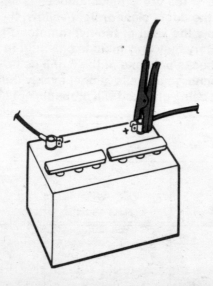

⚠DANGER

A spark could ignite gasses causing an explosion or fire.

SERVICING ENGINE AND DRIVE
SPARK PLUGS

The gasoline engines used to power inboard motors, outboard motors, generator sets, automobiles, trucks and recreational vehicles, all use spark plugs to ignite the combustionable mixture. If a spark plug does not deliver a spark, the mixture for that cylinder will not be ignited. Failure of part of the spark plugs of multicylinder engines will result in problems ranging from rough operation to failure to start. Of course other parts of the ignition can also cause problems, but since the spark plugs operate in such a hostile environment, it is often the cause of not starting or poor running.

At least once each year the ignition systems should be included in a "tune-up" to provide efficient engine operation and lessen the possibility of a breakdown. Depending on the complexity of the tune-up procedure, the tune-up may require a professional mechanic or may be performed by someone with the required mechanical expertise. Tune-up specifications are available in service and maintenance manuals or often from the operator's manual for the specific equipment.

The most frequent problem is spark plug fouling due to an accumulation of oil and fuel on the spark plug electrodes. When an engine begins to miss or is difficult to start, the first item to check is the spark plugs (presuming it is not out of gas).

▲CAUTION

Do not operate the engine with the battery disconnected or removed. Most systems use the battery for more than just starting. The charging system for instance will probably interpret zero battery voltage as a need to charge at the maximum possible rate. Usually this results in damaged alternator and regulator.

Identification

Spark plugs are manufactured in a variety of sizes, shapes and specifications to conform to different engine designs and applications. The large variety of available plugs also makes it easy to install the WRONG spark plug, which can result in serious engine damage.

Each spark plug manufacturer has a unique code to identify the characteristics of its spark plugs, and application charts are available from the manufacturers and distributors.

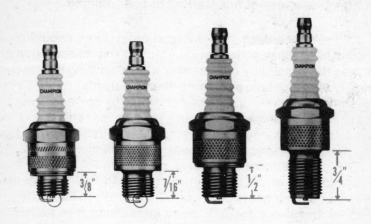

THREAD SIZE. The end of the spark plug that screws into the cylinder head is threaded. The diameter indicates the thread size — 10mm, 14mm, 18mm, ⅞-inch, etc. *Thread pitch* is an established industry standard but it may be indicated differently, as in "½-inch pipe."

SEALING TYPE. If a special sealing washer is used to seal between the spark plug and cylinder head, the surface of the head and plug must both be flat. Another method of sealing is with a carefully controlled angled (tapered) seat on the spark plug and a matching seat machined into the cylinder head. Never attempt to install a spark plug with the incorrect type of sealing.

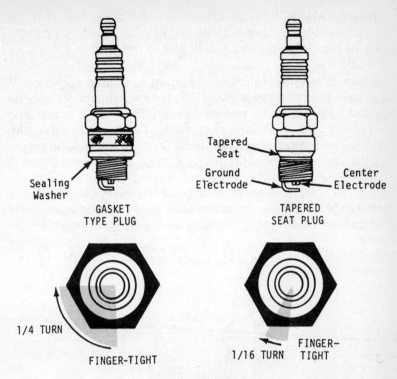

GASKET
TYPE PLUG

TAPERED
SEAT PLUG

Sealing
Washer

Tapered
Seat

Ground
Electrode

Center
Electrode

1/4 TURN

FINGER-TIGHT

1/16 TURN

FINGER-
TIGHT

TIGHTENING WITH
SOCKET WRENCH

A sealing washer is used only when the surface of the cylinder head and the spark plug are both flat (left). A cylinder head with a tapered seat requires a spark plug with a carefully controlled angled seat (right) that matches the angle machined into the cylinder head.

REACH. The length of the threaded section measured from the gasket or tapered seat to the combustion chamber end of the thread is the *reach dimension.* Some standard reaches are ⅜-inch, 7/16-inch, 0.492-inch, ½-inch and ¾-inch; however, spark plugs with different reaches are available. An engine can be damaged by a spark plug with the wrong reach even if the reach is very close.

Spark plugs with various reaches are available. Small engines usually are equipped with a 3/8-inch reach spark plug. Circled electrodes illustrate the difference between plugs normally used in two-stroke cycle engines (left) and four-stroke engines.

HEAT RANGE. Heat generated during combustion is trans-ferred from the center electrode and insulator to the plug shell, then to the cylinder head and finally to the engine-cooling air or liquid coolant.

Spark plug temperature is important to engine operation. If the spark plug surface is TOO HOT, the fuel-air mixture may be ignited before a spark occurs (pre-ignition). If the spark plug surface is TOO COLD, the plug will foul with unburned or par-tially burned combustion products. Some manufacturers iden-tify the spark plug heat ranges by a range of numbers. Be care-ful, however, because the numbers indicating cold to hot range may run from small to large *or* from large to small. The heat range codes are unique to each spark plug manufacturer and cannot be compared directly with plugs from another.

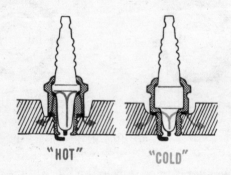

"HOT"   "COLD"

SPECIAL FEATURES. Engine design and application to specific equipment will usually require that the spark plug in-corporate some special features. Some of the features may in-clude electrode shape or material, nonstandard hex size and special radio interference protection. The equipment manufac-turer considers each special feature of the recommended spark plug to be necessary, and installing plugs with different features is discouraged.

SELECTION. Check the appropriate engine service manual, operators book or spark plug application chart to find the specific spark plug the manufacturer recommends. If the removed spark plug is different from the recommended one, find out why. Slight differences in heat range may be desirable because of operating conditions, such as for lighter-than-normal load or constant overload.

Removing And Installing Spark Plugs

The engine should be allowed to cool before removing spark plugs. Pull the wire connector from the spark plug, being careful not to damage the wire or connector. Grip the boot at the connector and twist until loosened, then pull connector away from spark plug. Some spark plugs may be hard to reach, but do not pull on the wire. Grip and pull only on the connector boot. Be careful not to slip and injure yourself when connector releases from spark plug.

Use the correct size spark plug wrench to turn the spark plug counterclockwise approximately 1 turn. Apply steady pressure to wrench until plug loosens. Use penetrating oil if plug is difficult to remove. Forcing a spark plug that is seized will nearly always damage threads in cylinder head.

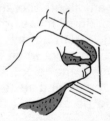

Remove wrench, then clean spark plug and pocket around plug. It is important to remove all of the dirt which could either fall into engine cylinder or onto sealing surface for spark plug. Clean the area with a brush and by blowing with compressed air. Remove the spark plug completely, then use a cloth to clean the threaded opening for spark plug. Be sure that gasket is removed with plug, if so equipped.

If spark plug is difficult to remove by hand, after loosening, carbon may have builtup in threaded area of cylinder head. Inspect the threads carefully and clean using a thread-chaser tool before installing a new plug. If spark plug has seized or threads are damaged, repair damage before installing new spark plug.

Check the appropriate engine service manual, operator's book, spark plug application chart or parts supplier to find the type of spark plug recommended by the manufacturer. If the removed spark plug is different than the one recommended, find out why. All spark plugs are not alike and installation of the wrong plug can damage the engine.

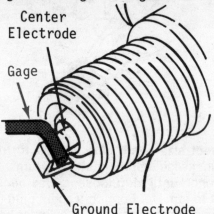

Center Electrode

Gage

Ground Electrode

Inspect the new spark plug for correct electrode gap. Check the engine service manual or operator's book for recommended electrode gap, then measure gap between center electrode and ground electrode by inserting the correct thickness of gage. Gap is correct when the gage drags slightly as it is pulled between the electrodes. Change gap, if necessary, by bending the ground electrode slightly. If the gap is nearly zero, check to be sure that the plug has not been dropped and damaged.

Install the spark plug by hand into the threaded hole until snug, then use a wrench to finish tightening. Check the engine service manual for recommended torque. Spark plugs with **new** gaskets should usually be tightened ¼ turn after seating by hand. Spark plugs with tapered seat (no gasket) should usually be tightened 1/16 turn after seating by hand. Do not overtighten as the threads in the engine can be damaged.

Special Notes

Damaged threads in cylinder head are usually caused by improper spark plug installation. Aluminum cylinder heads are more easily damaged than cast iron and therefore more care should be exercised when installing plugs in aluminum. The following precautions should always be observed, especially when servicing spark plugs which are installed in aluminum cylinder heads.

1. Always cool engine before removing or installing spark plugs. Because of the different expansion rate, the threads of the spark plug and the threads in the cylinder head are distorted when Hot. The expansion of aluminum cylinder heads is much different than steel spark plugs.
2. Remove and inspect any spark plug which is difficult to install. Be careful not to cross thread spark plug, especially into the soft threads of an aluminum cylinder head. Inspect spark plug for bent or damaged threads. Use a thread-chaser tool to clean threads in cylinder head.
3. Use caution when removing spark plug that is difficult to turn. First, be sure that engine has completely cooled. Use penetrating oil and work cautiously, first loosening, then tightening small amounts until spark plug is removed. Finally, be prepared to accomplish the machining necessary to repair the destroyed threads in the cylinder head.

49

4. Tighten spark plugs to the recommended torque. Overtightening a steel spark plug in an aluminum cylinder head will easily distort and damage the softer aluminum threads. Insufficient tightening may permit burning gasses to escape past the threads and sealing surface which can also easily destroy the cylinder head threads.
5. Some manufacturers recommend the use of anti-seize compound on threads of spark plugs used in aluminum cylinder heads.
6. Make sure that correct spark plug is installed. Plug with incorrect thread length may protrude past threads in cylinder head permitting carbon to accumulate on spark plug threads. Subsequent removal of spark plug will require carbon coated threads of plug to pass through and damage the threads in cylinder head.

Servicing Plugs

The appearance of a spark plug will be altered by use, and an examination of the plug tip can contribute useful information which may assist in obtaining better spark plug life. It must be remembered that the contributing factors differ in 2 stroke and 4 stroke engine operation and although the appearance of two spark plugs may be similar, the corrective measures may depend on whether the engine is of 2 stroke or 4 stroke design.

Normal plug appearance in 4 stroke cycle engine. Insulator is light tan to gray in color and electrodes are not burned. Renew plug at regular intervals as recommended by engine manufacturer.

Appearance of 4 stroke cycle spark plug indicating wet fouling; a wet, black oily film is over entire firing end of plug. Cause may be oil getting by worn valve guides, worn oil rings or plugged breather or breather valve in tappet chamber.

Appearance of 4 stroke cycle spark plug indicating cold fouling. Cause of cold fouling may be use of a too-cold plug, excessive idling or light loads, carburetor choke out of adjustment, defective spark plug wire or boot, carburetor adjusted too "rich" or low engine compression.

Appearance of 4 stroke cycle spark plug indicating over heating. Check for plugged cooling fins, bent or damaged blower housing, engine being operated without all shields in place or other causes of engine overheating. Also can be caused by too lean a fuel-air mixture if spark plug is not tightened properly.

Normal appearance of plug removed from a 2 stroke cycle engine. Insulator is light tan to gray in color, few deposits are present and electrodes are not burned.

Appearance of plug from 2 stroke cycle engine indicating wet fouling. A damp or wet black carbon coating is formed over entire firing end. Could be caused by a too-cold plug, excessive idling, improper fuel-lubricating oil mixture or carburetor adjustment too rich.

Appearance of plug from 2 stroke cycle engine indicating overheating. Insulator has gray or white blistered appearance and electrodes may be burned. Could be caused by use of a too-hot plug, carburetor adjustment too lean, "sticky" piston rings, engine overloaded, or cooling fins plugged causing engine to run too hot.

Spark plugs can sometimes be cleaned, but the easiest and best way of ensuring the best possible condition is to install a new spark plug of correct type.

Spark plug electrode gap can be changed by bending the ground electrode. Refer to manufacturer's specifications for desired clearance between the center electrode and the side (ground) electrode. Faces of electrodes should be parallel. Special tools are available for measuring the gap and bending the ground electrode.

ENGINE OIL

Engines are lubricated using a variety of methods; however, all must be lubricated. Check with a local dealer for explanation of what happens when an operator **doesn't make sure** that the engine has enough oil.

Some 2 stroke engines used to power boats and other recreational equipment are lubricated by mixing oil with the gasoline. The engine doesn't check to see if your intentions were pure. If the wrong type or wrong amount of oil is used, the engine will let you know that it wasn't and repair is sure to cost more than the oil.

Attempts to operate any engine with little or no oil is sure to result in damage to the engine. Operating with even a slightly reduced amount of oil will overheat the remaining oil very quickly. The excessive heat will reduce the lubricating quality of the oil, which in turn increases friction causing even more heat to be absorbed by the oil. The spiral often ends with dramatic damage to the engine, but serious damage has probably occurred even if unnoticed.

Engine damage can result from lack of proper lubrication, caused by overheating even **with** the recommended amount of oil. High oil temperature may be caused by the engine overheating from not enough coolant, blocked cooling air passages or a variety of other problems which could have been prevented by proper owner maintenance.

Heavy loads including trailer pulling will increase engine heat and subsequently will result in higher oil temperature. Many late model engines already operate at high temperature to assist emission control and to improve fuel mileage and additional heat may cause serious damage. Installation of trailer pulling packages, which include increased oil capacity and/or oil coolers, is recommended if not included in standard design.

SELECTING RIGHT TYPE OF OIL

Early in the development of modern gasoline and diesel engines, it was obvious that certain qualities in the lubricating oil would increase engine life. In 1911 the SAE established guidelines for grading engine oil viscosity. In 1947 the API adopted a classification system that divided oils into three groups to indicate straight mineral oil, oil containing oxidation inhibitors and heavy-duty oil, which included oxidation inhibitors and detergent-dispersant additives. These early grades and classifications are still being refined and expanded to meet the demands of modern engines.

Each container of oil is marked with the SAE and API service classification so that people servicing and operating equipment can easily select an oil that meets the needs of the engine as determined by the manufacturer.

SAE viscosity grades indicate the resistance to flow at specific temperatures. Standard numbers (5W, 10W, 20W, 20, 30, 40 and 50) range from very thin oil suitable for engine operation in very low temperatures to thicker oils suitable for higher temperatures. Multiviscosity oils are those that test within the range of one of the W grades at −18°C and also within the range of non-W grade when tested at 100°C.

Select an oil viscosity suitable for the ambient temperature. In summer, consider the highest ambient temperature; in winter, consider the lowest expected temperature. In winter, the oil must be thin enough to permit easy starting. Check the engine or equipment operator's book for the SAE viscosity grades the manufacturer recommends.

The API classifications describe the type of service and coincide with ASTM-established test methods that help engine manufacturers determine which oil should be used. The chart explains the current API classification letter designation codes.

Letter Designation	API Engine Service Description

Formerly for Utility Gasoline and Diesel Engine Service

SA

Service typical of older engines operated under such mild conditions that the protection afforded by compounded oils is not required. This category has no performance requirements and oils in this category should not be used in any engine unless specifically recommended by the equipment manufacturer.

Minumum-Duty Gasoline Engine Service

SB

Service typical of older gasoline engines operated under such mild conditions that only minimum protection afforded by compounding is desired. Oils designed for this service have been used since the 1930s and provide only antiscuff capability and resistance to oil oxidation and bearing corrosion. Oils in this category should not be used in any engine unless specifically recommended by the equipment manufacturer.

Letter Designation	API Engine Service Description

1964 Gasoline Engine Warranty Service

SC — Service typical of gasoline engines in 1964-1967 models of passenger cars and trucks operating under engine manufacturers' warranties in effect during those model years. Oil designed for this service provide control of high- and low-temperature deposits, wear, rust and corrosion in gasoline engines.

1968 Gasoline Engine Warranty Maintenance Service

SD — Service typical of gasoline engines in 1968 through 1979 models of passenger cars and some trucks operating under engine manufacturers' warranties in effect during those model years. Also may apply to certain 1971 and/or later models, as specified (or recommended) in the operator's book. Oils designed for this service provide more protection than Category SC oils against high- and low-temperature engine deposits, wear, rust and corrosion in gasoline engines. API Engine Service Category SD oil may be used when API Engine Service Category SC is recommended.

1972 Gasoline Engine Warranty Maintenance Service

SE — Service typical of gasoline engines in passenger cars and some trucks beginning with 1972 and certain 1971 models operating under engine manufacturers' warranties. Oils designed for this service provide more protection than Category SD oils against oil oxidation, high-temperature engine deposits, rust and corrosion in gasoline engines. API Engine Service Category SE oil may be used when either Category SC or SD is recommended.

Letter Designation	API Engine Service Description

1980 Gasoline Engine Warranty Maintenance Service

SF

Service typical of gasoline engines in passenger cars and some trucks beginning with the 1980 model operating under engine manufacturers' recommended maintenance procedures. Oils developed for this service provide increased oxidation stability and improved anti-wear performance over Category SE oils. These oils also provide protection against engine deposits, rust and corrosion. Oils meeting API Service Category SF may be used when Category SC, SD or SE oil is recommended.

Light-Duty Diesel Engine Service

CA for Diesel Engine Service

Service typical of diesel engines operated in mild to moderate duty with high-quality fuels. Oils designed for this service provide protection from bearing corrosion and from ring belt deposits in some naturally aspirated diesel engines when using fuels of such quality that they impose no unusual requirements for wear and deposit protection. Widely used in the late 1940s and 1950s but should not be used in any engine unless specifically recommended by the equipment manufacturer.

Moderate Duty Diesel Engine Service

CB for Diesel Engine Service

Service typical of diesel engines operated in mild to moderate duty, but with lower quality fuels that necessitate more protection from wear and deposits. Oils designed for this service were introduced in 1949. Such oils provide necessary protection from bearing corrosion and from high-temperature deposits in normally aspirated diesel engines with higher sulfur fuels.

Letter Designation	API Engine Service Description

Moderate-Duty Diesel and Gasoline Engine Service

CC for Diesel Engine Service

Service typical of lightly supercharged diesel engines operated in moderate to severe duty and has included certain heavy-duty gasoline engines. Oils designed for this service were introduced in 1961 and used in many trucks and in industrial and construction equipment and farm tractors. These oils provide protection from high temperature deposits in lightly supercharged diesels and also from rust, corrosion and low-temperature deposits in gasoline engines.

Severe-Duty Diesel Engine Service

CD for Diesel Engine Service

Service typical of supercharged diesel engines in high-speed, high-output duty requiring highly effective control of wear and deposits. Oils designed for this service were introduced in 1955. They provide protection from bearing corrosion and from high-temperature deposits in supercharged diesel engines when using fuels of a wide quality range.

Early classifications ML, MM and MS are approximately like the later designations SA, SB and SC. Most engines that specify use of oils identified with SC, SD or (early) MS designation may safely use SE or SF oils. If the manufacturer specifies SA, SB, (early) ML or (early) MM designations, the additives in other oil classifications may be harmful and should not be used.

For 2 stroke engines, check with manufacturer for recommended type. Liquid cooled engines such as outboard engines operate at cooler temperatures than air cooled 2 stroke engines. Snowmobiles operate with different considerations and oil formulated for them probably won't be right either. Many equipment manufacturers market an oil to reduce confusion and to make sure that people who use their products can know which oil is OK.

MIXING GASOLINE AND OIL FOR TWO STROKE ENGINES

Two stroke engines used as outboard motors and other powered equipment are lubricated by oil mixed with the gasoline. The manufacturers carefully determine which type of oil and how much oil should be mixed with the gasoline to provide the most desirable operation, then list these mixing instructions in the operator's manual. Often two or more oil to gasoline ratios will be listed depending upon type of oil or severity of service. It is important to always follow the recommended mixing instructions, because mixing the wrong amount of oil or using the wrong type of oil can cause extensive engine damage. Too much oil can cause lower power, spark plug fouling and excessive carbon build up. Not enough oil will cause inadequate lubrication and will probably result in scuffing, seizure and other forms of damage.

⚠CAUTION

It is important to mix oil with gasoline for proper lubrication of 2 stroke engines designed for this type of lubrication; but, engines designed for operation with gasoline only will not operate properly if oil is mixed with the fuel. Be sure of manufacturer's fuel recommendation and fill tank ONLY with that type of fuel or mix. Storage tank should be marked to indicate if it contains gasoline and oil mix or gasoline only.

Some manufacturers recommend only regular gasoline and caution not to use low-lead, unleaded, premium gasoline, gasohol or other blends of gasoline, while other manufacturers may recommend using only low-lead gasoline. Follow the suggestions of the equipment manufacturer. NEVER use gasoline which has been stored for a long time or fluid which may not be gasoline.

Accurate measurement of gasoline and oil is necessary to ensure correct lubrication. Proper quantities of gasoline and oil for some of the more common mix ratios are listed below.

Ratio	Gasoline	Oil
10:1	.63 Gallon	½ Pint (237mL)
14:1	.88 Gallon	½ Pint (237mL)
16:1	1.00 Gallon	½ Pint (237mL)
20:1	1.25 Gallons	½ Pint (237mL)
30:1	1.88 Gallons	½ Pint (237mL)
32:1	2.00 Gallons	½ Pint (237mL)
50:1	3.13 Gallons	½ Pint (237mL)

Ratio	Gasoline	Oil
10:1	1 Gallon	.79 Pint (379mL)
14:1	1 Gallon	.57 Pint (270mL)
16:1	1 Gallon	.50 Pint (237mL)
20:1	1 Gallon	.40 Pint (189mL)
30:1	1 Gallon	.27 Pint (126mL)
32:1	1 Gallon	.25 Pint (118mL)
50:1	1 Gallon	.16 Pint (76mL)

When mixing, use a separate, approved safety container which is large enough to hold the desired amount of fuel with additional space for mixing. Pour about ½ of the required amount of gasoline into container, add the required amount of gasoline into container, add the required amount of oil, then shake vigorously until completely mixed. Pour remaining amount of gasoline into container, then complete mixing by shaking. Serious engine damage can be caused by incomplete mixing. NEVER attempt to mix gasoline and oil in the equipment fuel tank.

SAFETY HINT

All fuel is potentially dangerous. If fuel wouldn't burn, it wouldn't be used as engine fuel. Always be careful. Fire requires three things:

1. Oxygen   2. Fuel   3. Ignition

Oxygen is in the air and fuel can be wood, paper, grass, leaves, rubber, gasoline or diesel fuel. A match will ignite paper easily and just about any spark or flame can be used to ignite gasoline or diesel fuel, especially when you least suspect a fire.

Always observe the following:

Use only properly marked, approved safety containers for mixing and storing fuel. Make sure container is in good condition.

Mix fuel and oil and refuel only outdoors.

Stop engine and allow to cool before refueling.

Never smoke near equipment refueling area or where the odor of fuel is detected.

Avoid spilling fuel. Accidental spills should be cleaned completely before starting engine.

Observe safe procedures at all times.

— Use safety container for mixing and storing fuel.
— Handle gasoline and oil only in well ventilated area away from all flames, sparks and other ignition sources.
— Be careful not to spill fuel or overfill fuel tank. Wipe up any spilled fuel immediately.
— Don't fill fuel tank while engine is running.
— Leave some room for fuel to expand in the equipment fuel tank when filling. Do not fill tank to overflowing.

Draining Inboard Engine Oil And Changing Filter

Consult the specific engine operator's manual to find the manufacturer's recommended oil and filter change interval. Engine oil and the system filter should be changed more frequently than recommended if the engine is subjected to severe operating conditions such as extended slow speed operation, short trips, cold temperatures or if the engine is excessively worn. oil should be changed seasonally even if operated very little.

Draining oil from the bottom of an engine crankcase is difficult when the engine is located in the small enclosed compartment of many boats. If oil is spilled, clean up the mess immediately, because it is dangerous as well as unsightly. Commercial bilge cleaning solvents are available which hold oil in suspension for easier, more complete, safe cleaning.

The oil dipstick tube of some engines extends to the bottom of the crankcase so that oil can be drawn (sucked) from the crankcase using a hose and pump attached to the top of the dipstick tube. Manual and powered pumps are available, but be sure that dipstick tube is designed for this method of oil removal.

Oil suction systems are also available with a small diameter tube which can be inserted through the dipstick tube to the bottom of the crankcase. Be sure that suction tube extends to the bottom of the crankcase and that tube does not become clogged while drawing oil from crankcase.

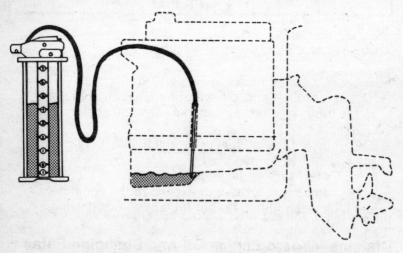

The oil suctioning unit shown is available from VACULA AUTOMOTIVE PRODUCTS, 45 Earhart Drive, Suite 106, Williamsville, NY 14221.

If oil is drained by removing a plug from the bottom of the engine crankcase, be careful to select a container that will hold all of the oil and which can still be removed from below the engine without spilling. Flexible plastic oil drain bags ease draining and are available from several vendors.

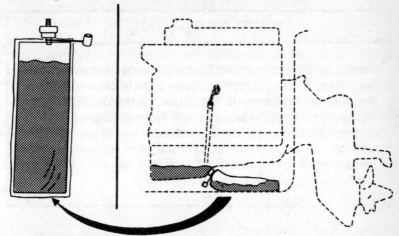

The oil draining system shown includes a special quick change automatic valve, which is installed in place of the drain plug, and flexible, disposable bags for containing the drained oil. The system shown is produced by Sta-Lube, Inc., P.O. Box 5746, Rancho Domingues, CA 90224.

The oil is filtered by a disposable unit that should be removed and discarded. The filter traps dirt and other impurities that are circulating, suspended in the engine lubricating oil. Modern oils are formulated to hold dirt, carbon and other impurities in suspension so that the filter can trap these small particles. Consult the specific engine operator's manual for recommended oil filter change interval. The filters are provided with a bypass valve which permits oil circulation in the event that the filter is plugged with dirt; however, the by-passed oil is no longer filtered. Before the old filter is completely filled, the old filter should be removed and discarded, then a new filter should be installed. The cost of the disposable filters is slight and the filter is usually very easy to change.

To remove the filter, use a suitable wrench to turn the filter counterclockwise. Use a suitable container to catch spilled oil and the old filter. A plastic bag may be convenient when changing the oil filter. Use a clean cloth to wipe the surface contacted by the oil filter gasket. Make sure that surface is clean and not damaged and that old seal (or gasket) is not stuck to the surface.

HELPFUL HINT

Select an oil filter wrench that will remove the most stubborn filter from your engine. No wrench is clearly superior for all applications. If the filter is stuck, it may be necessary to rotate the wrench several degrees before enough force is applied to unscrew the filter. Select a wrench that grips firmly, but also be sure that wrench can be turned through a large arc within the limited space available in the engine compartment.

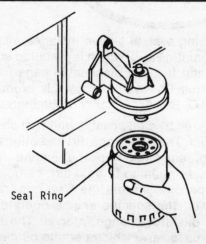

Seal Ring

Coat the seal of the new oil filter with new engine oil before installing. The new oil filter must be filled with oil before oil will circulate to the engine's bearings. Some new oil can be poured into the new oil filter before installing to reduce the chance for damage caused by lack of lubrication. If the filter is installed in a nearly upright position, the filter can be almost filled with oil. Even if located in horizontal or inverted position, the filter can hold enough oil to assist earlier lubrication.

Fill the engine with the proper amount of new oil of the type recommended by the equipment manufacturer. The correct type of oil depends upon engine design, temperature and type of service. The "BEST" oil will not be the same for all applications. Check to be sure oil level is correct, then start engine. Check to be sure oil pressure quickly reaches correct pressure and that oil is not leaking. Operate engine for about 5 minutes, while checking for leaks. Stop engine and repair any leaks, then fill to correct level and recheck if any leaks were discovered. Check oil level after engine has been stopped and allowed to drain back into crankcase, about 5 minutes. Be sure oil level is exactly correct, then record when the oil (and filter) was changed so that the proper interval can be maintained.

Inspect the drained oil for any easily identifiable indications of problems. If the oil is heavily contaminated, the interval between oil and filter changes should be reduced. Dilution of the oil by water, anti-freeze or fuel is probably caused by mechanical damage which should be repaired immediately. Contamination by larger chunks of metal, gaskets, "O" rings or other identifiable engine parts should be quickly corrected.

DIESEL FUEL

Diesel fuel lubricates and cools the fuel injection components of the engine in addition to sustaining combustion. Use only CLEAN, HIGH QUALITY fuel of CORRECT GRADE to protect the expensive precision-made components from wear and damage.

Fuel Grade

The American Society for Testing Materials (ASTM) has adopted certain grade standards to identify different diesel fuels. Each grade of fuel will meet the needs for certain engines in certain operating conditions. Most power equipment manufacturers consider only grades 1-D and 2-D satisfactory for use.

Grade 1-D is more volatile than 2-D. Most manufacturers recommend 1-D for cold temperatures, wide variations in load, frequent speed changes, long periods of idling with low load, and high altitude operation.

Grade 2-D is recommended for warm ambient temperatures, heavy load, high speeds and lower altitudes. The requirements are often conflicting, making selection difficult. Follow the selection guide defined by the manufacturer in the operators manual for the specific equipment.

Cetane Number

Cold starting, warm-up, roughness, acceleration, carbon deposits and exhaust smoke can be affected by the ignition quality of the fuel, which is measured by the cetane method. The minimum cetane number specified by the ASTM for both 1-D and 2-D is 40. The engine manufacturer may suggest fuel with a higher cetane number at low ambient temperature and high altitude. Check with your fuel supplier for availability of fuel with higher cetane ratings.

Contamination

The engine manufacturer often specifies limits of sulfur, water and sediment in the fuel. Usually these are within other regulated limits for fuel sold commercially; however, be sure these limits are not exceeded in the fuel when it is injected into the combustion chamber.

Improper storage and handling can contaminate good fuel. Diesel fuel contains some sulfur and water. Combining the two forms sulfuric acid, which will etch metal parts.

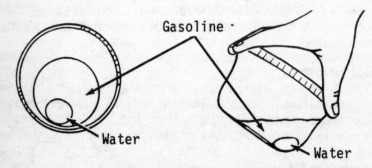

Gasoline

Water

Water

Condensation of moisture in diesel fuel storage tanks occurs more easily than in tanks for gasoline because the more volatile gasoline vapors provide some resistance to the entrance of moisture-laden air. The moisture condenses inside the tank and the water droplets then run into the diesel fuel.

Fill the fuel tanks at the end of each day to reduce air space for condensation. Allow enough time for water and contaminants to settle and drain water traps at the beginning of each day. Inspect fuel filters often and change them before they become plugged.

Do not store diesel fuel in galvanized containers because the fuel may dissolve the zinc coating, which can then remain in solution until deposited in the pump or injectors. Fuel additives often contain alcohol or another solvent that can dissolve plastic parts. Use additives with extreme caution — only after considering the engine manufacturer's recommendations.

Cloud Point

When the temperature is cold enough, diesel fuel forms wax crystals that will not pass through filters. The temperature at which the crystals form is. identified as the *cloud point* because the fuel will appear cloudy. Use fuel with a cloud point at least 10°F (12°C) lower than the lowest anticipated ambient temperature to prevent plugging of the filters in cold weather. Some additives can be safely used to lower the cloud point, but use extreme caution and follow manufacturers' guidelines. Never add alcohol or gasoline to diesel fuel.

Fuel Storage

Diesel fuel should be stored carefully to protect it from contaminants, using large, permanent storage tanks. These permanent storage tanks should be maintained carefully. Fuel from these tanks should be filtered as it is transferred to equipment tanks.

Water requires a long time to settle to the bottom of diesel fuel, necessitating the fuel to stand 12 to 24 hours before the water can be drained.

Observe the following precautions:

☐ Don't ever transfer fuel in an open container.

☐ Don't knock dirt into the tank while filling. Clean the cap before removing it.

☐ Don't store diesel fuel in a galvanized container. The fuel reacts with and dissolves the galvanized coating, later depositing this material in the filters and engine.

☐ Don't store diesel fuel in containers that were previously used for gasoline or other solvent unless the containers are very carefully cleaned. Fine rust and dirt, which will quickly settle out of gasoline, will mix readily with the diesel fuel and cause damage.

☐ Drain the water trap and service filter as suggested by the manufacturer.

☐ If necessary to use smaller containers to transport fuel, make sure the portable containers are clean before filling them with fuel.

PROPELLERS

A propeller is designed to move a boat through the water in somewhat the same manner that a wood screw passes through a piece of wood. Propellers are rated by diameter, pitch and the number of blades. Diameter is the distance across a circle described by the blade tips and pitch is the forward thrust imparted in one revolution of the propeller.

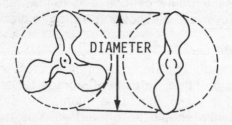

The correct propeller diameter is determined by motor design, especially the items of horsepower and propeller shaft gear ratio, and should usually not be changed from that recommended by the manufacturer. Propeller pitch is more nearly comparable to the transmission gear ratio of an automobile and should be individually selected to suit the conditions of boat design and usage. Propeller blade number affects efficiency and vibration level. The lower the blade number, the higher the efficiency and the higher the vibration. Because of this, most propellers are made with three blades. The efficiency difference between two- and three-blade propellers is thought not to be as important as the vibrational difference. Efficiency is greatest when the propeller operates with minimal slippage. Actual amount of accepted slippage is usually dependent upon the type of application. Normal slippage on a racing hull may be as low as 10%, while a slow speed hull may normally be allowed 50-60%.

With the wide range of propeller applications, various propeller types and propeller design features are used to provide the best performance for the intended application. The following describes some propeller types and various design features.

Constant Pitch

A constant pitch (flat blade) propeller operates efficiently only at relatively slow rotative speeds. Above a certain critical speed, water is moved from the blade area faster than additional water can flow into the area behind the blades, causing "cavitation" and erratic behavior. The extreme turbulence and shock waves caused by cavitation rapidly reduces operating efficiency.

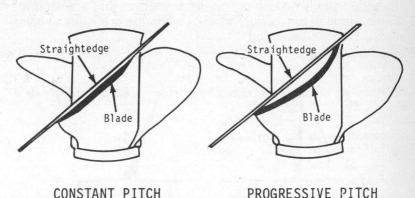

CONSTANT PITCH   PROGRESSIVE PITCH

Progressive Pitch

The progressive pitch propeller has an assigned pitch number that is the average pitch over the entire blade length. The propeller is designed to improve performance at higher speeds or when the propeller breaks the water surface.

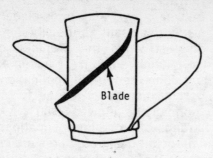

CUPPED BLADE

Cupped Blade

A cupped propeller is a propeller that has the trailing edge of the blades curled outward from the boat. The cupped blades help the propeller to hold water better when operating in a cavitating or ventilating condition (ventilation is defined in a later paragraph). This will allow the engine or drive unit to be further adjusted for optimum performance. Cupping will normally add one-half inch to one inch of pitch, which will usually cause engine full throttle rpm to be reduced by 150-300 rpm. Cupping usually has no benefit on propellers that are used in applications of heavy duty work or when the propeller always remains fully submerged.

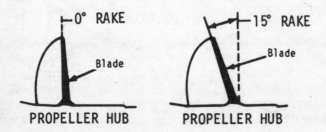

Blade Rake

Blade rake is the amount the blade slants back towards the aft end of the propeller. Most standard propellers are raked from 0-20 degrees. Generally the higher rake angle will improve the ability of the propeller to operate in a cavitating or ventilating condition.

Selection

Proper propeller selection is one of the most important factors affecting boat and motor performance. The engine manufacturer, boat builder or dealer will provide a propeller that they believe offers the best overall performance and the engine should reach maximum operating rpm range at full throttle under normal load with this propeller. It may not be optimum design, pitch or material for a specific operation, but can certainly be used as a base for making another selection.

An accurate tachometer is necessary for determining engine speed. If the boat's permanently installed tachometer is to be used, first check the accuracy, especially at higher rpm. Operate the boat with normal load at full throttle and observe the engine speed.

DANGER

Use care and safe boating practices while operating at maximum speed. DO NOT endanger yourself or others while checking propeller selection. Also, observe safe limits of engine speed suggested by engine manufacturer to avoid overspeeding and damage.

If engine speed will not reach the high rpm range suggested by the engine manufacturer, the engine is being overloaded and is not able to operate efficiently.

If engine speed will exceed the high rpm limit suggested by the engine manufacturer, serious engine damage can result. Boat performance is probably less than optimum as well.

Special applications such as water skiing, high speed performance or carrying a heavy load may require a change to a different propeller to attain the best possible performance. It is always best to carry a spare propeller in case of damage while away from port. Some boaters have two (or more) different types of propellers so that the boat's performance can be changed to match the type of use. The alternate propeller can be used as a spare. Change the propeller if damaged. Imbalance caused by a damaged propeller can quickly damage the drive.

Propellers are usually constructed of aluminum, bronze, plastic or stainless steel. Aluminum propellers are most commonly used on outboards and stern drives. Bronze propellers are commonly used on inboard applications. Plastic propellers are primarily used on low horsepower engine applications. Stainless steel propellers are popular on high performance applications.

⚠CAUTION

It is not a good practice to use bronze propellers in salt water applications due to galvanic corrosion.

Select a propeller or propellers that matches the requirements of the boat, drive and the type of operation. Remember it is extremely important that the engine reaches manufacturer's rated rpm at full throttle operation. Only then will you get optimum performance out of your engine. **Use a good-quality tachometer to measure rpm** and change the type of propeller if needed. Note the following is important to remember:

1. Insufficient pitch will cause engine to overspeed. A low pitched propeller will usually allow the boat to get on plane quicker, but reduced top speed, poor fuel economy and accelerated engine wear could result.

2. Too much pitch will cause engine to "lug" and engine speed **cannot** reach recommended rpm level. When water skiing or carrying a heavy load, a lower pitch propeller may be required.

TRAILERING
TOW VEHICLE
Requirements

If you plan to trailer your boat with the vehicle you now own, be sure to consult with an authorized dealer or the manufacturer of the tow vehicle to be sure that safe limits are not exceeded. Newer vehicles, especially those with a lock-up clutch integral with the automatic transmission's torque converter, may not be able to tow more than about 1500 pounds. Extensive damage to the transmission and other parts of the drive system are never convenient, but failure while trying to pull a boat and trailer out of the water and up a steep ramp can be dangerous.

If you are buying a new vehicle to tow your trailer, you should follow the recommendations of the auto or truck manufacturer in making your selection. All the major auto manufacturers have studied the special needs of their vehicles for towing use and have printed brochures to help you properly match the tow vehicle equipment to your particular sized trailer.

Among optional items which may be important for optimum performance are:

a. Drive axle with more reduction than standard
b. Increased engine cooling system capacity
c. Additional cooler for automatic transmission fluid
d. Alternator and battery with increased capacity
e. Suspension system capable of carrying increased load
f. Tire size or rating suitable for additional weight
g. Heavy duty brake system

The auto or truck manufacturer may not have optional equipment available that is needed to safely pull heavier boats and trailers. Speciality equipment manufacturers or dealers may also be a source for heavy duty modifications, but use caution. Some modifications may void vehicle manufacturer's warranty.

Some vehicles just can't be made or modified to pull or stop heavy loads safely. Remember that it is easier to back a boat down a launching ramp than it is to drive up a steep ramp pulling a boat and trailer from the water. It is also more difficult to stop a vehicle pulling a heavy load and trailer. Some car and truck manufacturers suggest that trailers with a loaded weight of over 1,000 lbs. should be equipped with trailer brakes of adequate size.

If the tow vehicle is always having trouble and overloading is suspected, check with a reputable dealer or other authority.

Even with a properly equipped vehicle, try to avoid any type of driving that will result in panic stops or rapid lane changes. Also try to avoid situations that will overheat your vehicle's engine, automatic transmission or clutch.

HITCHES

Hitches commonly used to pull trailers are divided into four classes.

Class I—can be used for trailers with gross weight less than 2000 lbs. and tongue weight 10-15% of the Gross Trailer Weight. This hitch class may be either weight carrying or weight distributing (equalizing) type.

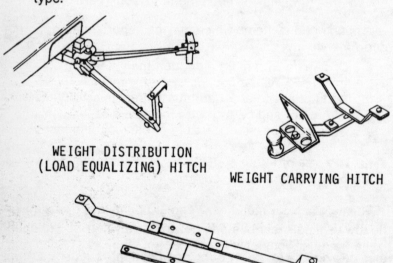

WEIGHT DISTRIBUTION
(LOAD EQUALIZING) HITCH

WEIGHT CARRYING HITCH

WEIGHT CARRYING HITCH

Class II—can be used for trailers with gross weight of 2001 through 3500 lbs. and tongue weight 10-15% of the Gross Trailer Weight. This hitch class may be either weight carrying or weight distributing (equalizing) type.

Class III—can be used for trailers with gross weight of 3501 through 5000 lbs. and tongue weight 15% of the Gross Trailer Weight. This hitch class must be of the weight distributing (equalizing) type.

Class IV—can be used for trailers with gross weight of more than 5000 lbs. and tongue weight should be 15% of the Gross Trailer Weight. This hitch class must be of the weight distributing (equalizing) type and must have anti-sway device.

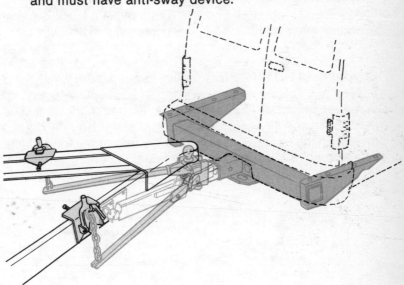

Weight carrying hitches are often attached to or are part of the tow vehicle's rear bumper; however, they may be attached to the frame or body of the tow vehicle. Most weight carrying hitches are marked with tongue weight limits which are considered by the manufacturer to be the maximum safe limit when properly installed. Never exceed this marked limit and, if not marked, never exceed 300 lbs. tongue weight for any weight carrying hitch. Weight carrying hitches should not be attached to any shock absorbing bumpers.

Weight distributing or "equalizer hitches" should be installed on the tow vehicle only by qualified personnel. The frame that is attached to the tow vehicle's frame or body is often called the "receiver" or "hitch receiver". It is important to attach this hitch receiver correctly to the tow vehicle by welding or bolting solidly to the vehicle frame or body. The hitch ball is attached to a hitch bar which is installed in the hitch receiver. The height and angle of the hitch ball should be the correct position as determined by the tow vehicle and the trailer. Adjustment of the hitch ball height and angle should be carefully accomplished by your dealer. Satisfaction with trailers is determined to a large extent by the proper selection, installation and adjustment of the hitch assembly.

Fifth wheel trailers are towed by vehicles which use special hitches usually mounted in the bed of a pick-up truck. Several variations are available and the dealer will help with both selection and installation.

EQUALIZER HITCHES. In addition to pulling the weight of a trailer, a tow vehicle must also support about 10% to 15% of the actual weight of the trailer at the hitch point. With a 6000 pound boat and trailer, this additional weight might be 900 pounds. This much weight added to the rear of the tow vehicle can alter balance and will probably result in poor steering control, poor braking control and can be potentially dangerous.

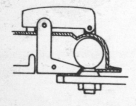

LATCH TYPE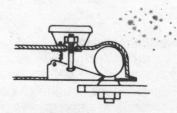

SCREW TYPE

Use of heavier springs, spring helpers or stiffer tires will not correct the basic out-of-balance condition. The problems from this condition are compounded when traveling over bumps and dips in the road. The balance problem is solved by addition of a suitably matched "equalizer hitch". The effect of an equalizer hitch is to distribute the hitch load equally between the front and rear tow vehicle axles and the trailer axle(s). Instead of the entire hitch weight sitting on the car's rear bumper, it is evenly distributed to the three axle areas and your tow vehicle can remain relatively level. This will not only give you better steering and brake control, but will keep your headlight beams down on the road where they belong.

Most hitch manufacturers offer hitches designed to handle trailers of various hitch weight classes. Your dealer will help you select the right size hitch required for your trailer's loaded weight.

SWAY CONTROLS. Heavy trailers should employ some type of sway control device. There are several types of these devices available operating on different principles such as friction, cam action and computer operated braking of the trailer wheels. Each has some advantages over the others as the manufacturer's literature will tell you. They will all decrease the sway effects induced by passing trucks and busses or strong side winds. They can make towing safer especially when driving under adverse conditions.

HITCH BALL. The diameter of the ball must be the correct size to fit the coupling of the trailer. The most popular size for smaller boat trailers is 2 inches in diameter; however, larger sizes may also be used on some trailers. Coupling of the trailer may be stamped with marking which indicates correct diameter of hitch ball.

If the hitch ball is too small, the trailer coupling may not latch far enough under the ball and the coupling may be able to lift away from ball. Also, if too small, the trailer will "rattle" around on the ball especially when starting up and stopping. Shock loads resulting from the loose fit of the ball may loosen the ball or some other part of the hitch and can break some part causing the trailer to fall. The trailer coupling can be permanently damaged by the wear caused by the improper size of ball.

If too large, the hitch ball will not fit into the coupling far enough to correctly engage the latch. Be especially careful of improper fit with trailers with heavy tongue weight. The static weight may be enough to hold the coupling on top of the ball just long enough to start moving, then the safety chains may be the last effort to avert a serious accident.

Always check the hitch and hitch ball for tightness. If the ball is loose, be sure that the stud for the ball is the correct size for hole in the hitch. Spacers are available to fill gap between the stud of a small hitch ball and the larger hole of a heavier class hitch.

⚠WARNING

Do not enlarge the hole in hitch. Size of hole is selected by the hitch manufacturer to help indicate limit. Recommended limits should also be stamped on the hitch.

Be sure hitch ball attaching stud is fitted with a lockwasher and tighten retaining nut sufficiently to prevent loosening. Apply grease to hitch ball and trailer coupler. Lubricate coupling lock mechanism. Tighten coupler latch enough to prevent coupling from accidently unhooking.

⚠WARNING

Be extremely cautious if coupler locking mechanism requires unusual adjustment. Adjustment beyond the normal range may indicate that ball is incorrect size or that ball is not properly positioned. The locking latch mechanism should be positioned approximately the same for all hitch balls that are the same size.

TRAILER

Optional Equipment

As delivered, the trailer is equipped to meet legal requirements where the unit was purchased. Laws will probably change and, because of the mobility of trailered boats, the location of the boat and trailer may also change. Be sure that your trailer meets or exceeds the current legal requirements.

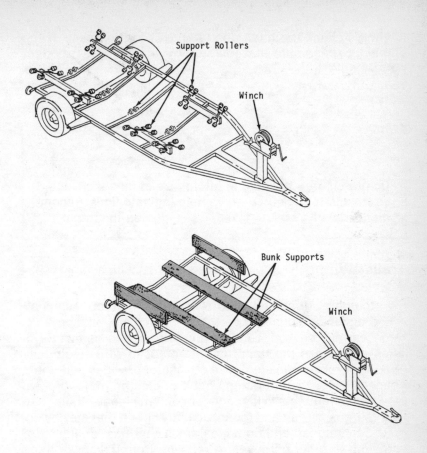

Support Rollers

Winch

Bunk Supports

Winch

The laws applicable to boat trailers and equipment usually offer only the minimum of safety protection. Additional equipment may be available which will provide better protection for the boat and which will make trailering easier and safer. Optional equipment which should be considered may include:

a. Larger wheels and tires
b. Additional axles
c. Better support for boat (bunks or more rollers)
d. Trailer brakes
e. Additional or improved lighting
f. Spare tire and wheel
g. Wheel bearing lubrication aids
h. Tongue jack

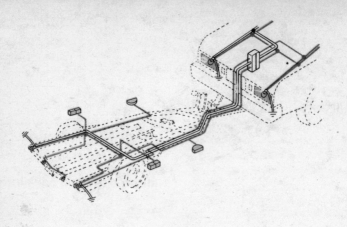

Trailer Wiring

Automobile, truck and boat trailer manufacturers nearly all follow a standard code for selecting wire colors, but some differences may be noticed. The four wire, inline connector is often used when the trailer is not equipped with electrically operated brakes. The eight wire connector provides additional connectors for the operating circuit of electric trailer brakes, stop light circuit that is independent of turn signals, trailer battery charging circuit and for an auxiliary circuit that may be used to separate left and right clearance/identification lights for signaling or other purposes. A red wire from the car or truck will probably be for battery charging circuit and a light green wire may be used for backup lights. Be sure to check wiring before causing damage to wiring.

A special adapter will probably be required if the tow vehicle has rear turn signals that are completely separate from the brake lights. The separate turn signal will usually have an amber lens and a red lens will be used for the stop light on each side. The adapter is available from most marine trailer dealers.

Older trailers may not comply with the standard wire colors, wires may be attached to the connector in different order and another style of connector may be used, but most boat trailers follow the accepted standards.

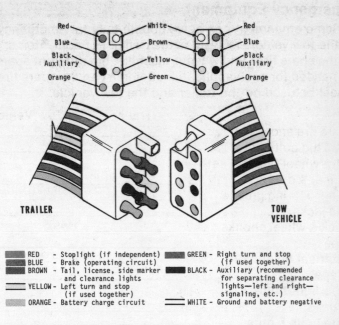

```
Red                White            Red
Blue               Brown            Blue
Black                               Black
Auxiliary          Yellow           Auxiliary
Orange             Green            Orange
```

TRAILER   **TOW VEHICLE**

RED   - Stoplight (if independent)
BLUE   - Brake (operating circuit)
BROWN - Tail, license, side marker
         and clearance lights
YELLOW - Left turn and stop
         (if used together)
ORANGE - Battery charge circuit

GREEN - Right turn and stop
        (if used together)
BLACK - Auxiliary (recommended
        for separating clearance
        lights—left and right—
        signaling, etc.)
WHITE - Ground and battery negative

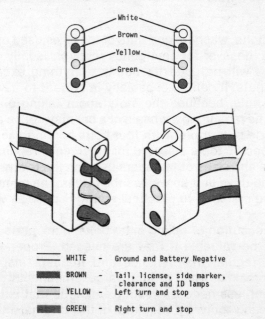

```
White
Brown
Yellow
Green
```

WHITE - Ground and Battery Negative
BROWN - Tail, license, side marker,
         clearance and ID lamps
YELLOW - Left turn and stop
GREEN - Right turn and stop

Emergency Equipment

Some equipment can serve double duty for emergency use of the tow vehicle as well as the trailer. For some items, such as the spare tires and wheels, a similar, but different spare will be needed for each application. Seldom can the spare tire and wheel be used on the trailer and the tow vehicle.

	Trailer	Tow Vehicle
Spare tire and wheel		
Extra lug bolts/nuts		
Extra wheel bearing set inner & outer		
Wheel bearing grease		
Axle jacks		
Block & wheel chocks		
Rope		
Electrical insulation tape		
Extra light bulbs & fuses		
Extra bolts & nuts		
Tools		

Extra bolts, washers and nuts of the sizes used on the trailer can be a lifesaver for emergency repairs. Usually only one or two sizes will be used for nearly everything except the lug bolts or nuts. It can be especially important to have extra lug bolts or nuts, because the story about taking one nut from each of the remaining 3 wheels of a car may not be as safe for a single axle boat trailer with four bolts holding each wheel.

The specific tools selected for emergency repairs should fit the types and sizes of fasteners used on the tow vehicle, boat, motor and drive unit as well as the trailer. The number of tools should be matched to practical storage space as well as your ability.

The precaution of taking extra bolts, nuts, parts, tools, etc., will only be valuable if they are needed. Proper service procedures, regular maintenance and frequent inspection will reduce break downs, making large amounts of emergency equipment less necessary. An example is that extra lug nuts will probably only be required if the original nuts are not tightened sufficiently.

HELPFUL HINT

Use of thread locking compound such as Permatex Bolt Guard or similar product will reduce rust on threads as well as keeping the threaded fasteners from loosening.

Safety Chains

There are different safety chain requirements for the various sizes. Heavier and/or additional chains with casehardened quick connect links may be desired. Always have the safety chains attached when towing. Install them so they do not restrict sharp turns, but tight enough so they do not drag on the road.

TYPICAL SINGLE
SAFETY CHAIN INSTALLATION

TYPICAL DOUBLE
SAFETY CHAIN INSTALLATION

Tires, Wheels And Bearings

The most common cause of trailer tire trouble is under inflation. Tires may gradually lose air while setting, so it is important to check tire air pressure **before** each trip. Pressure should be checked while cool and an under inflated tire will cause flexing that will heat the tire. Heat generated by normal flexing of a properly inflated tire may increase tire pressure approximately 6 to 9 psi. Do not bleed air from a hot tire.

Maximum safe air pressure suggested by the tire manufacturer is molded into the tire sidewall. Some trailer manufacturers suggest that correct tire air pressure is the recommended maximum that is molded into the tire. Air pressure that is too high will cause the trailer to ride rough and bounce, especially on rough roads. The rough ride can damage the boat and may also vibrate threaded parts enough to loosen some bolts. Additional trailer axles or optional larger wheel sizes will result in a smoother ride and will also be easier to tow.

Check wheel lug nuts or bolts before each trip and be sure that all are tight. Install new nuts or lug bolts if any are missing or damaged. Wheel wobble can be caused by nuts or bolts that are either too loose or too tight.

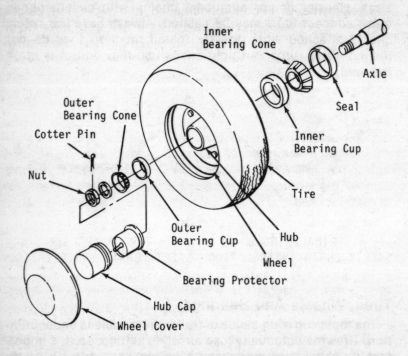

Lug nuts or bolts should be removed, cleaned, lubricated, then reinstalled occasionally to make sure that they can be removed if necessary. If not removed for several years, the nuts or bolts may rust and normal removal may be impossible. The side of a road with a flat tire is the wrong place and time to find that the lug nuts must be removed with a torch. Products are available that will protect the threads from rust without increasing the possibility of loosening.

⚠CAUTION

Be careful that lug nuts or bolts are kept tight. A normal response, especially after removing rusted lug bolts or nuts, is to oil or grease the threaded parts, then not tighten them sufficiently when reinstalling. Enough extra lug nuts or bolts to retain one trailer wheel may be carried for emergency.

Trailer wheels should be cleaned and repainted before damage interferes with removal of the wheel from the axle or the tire from the wheel. Rusted wheels may also allow air to escape from tire. Bent wheels may cause excessive tire wear, but will often shake the trailer, sometimes enough to damage the boat or trailer.

Check the temperature of the trailer wheel hubs everytime you stop while on a trip. If hub feels hot, remove, clean and inspect bearings. Wheel bearings should be cleaned and repacked with new grease at least twice each year, first in the spring before first use and again in the fall just before storing. Special marine lubricant or waterproof wheel bearing grease should be used.

Lights

All lights should be operating correctly. Check for correct operation before beginning each trip. Waterproof light assemblies may reduce failure caused by submersion, but cold water splashed onto a hot light bulb will probably cause the bulb to break. If lights are unplugged and allowed to cool before entering the water, the bulbs may break less often. Corrosion on the bulb or socket connectors can prevent the bulb from lighting. Corrosion may be reduced by coating the connectors with a suitable corrosion preventing solvent or silicone grease.

Clearance lights are usually the push in type that can be pulled from the sockets after snapping the lens cover off. Stop, tail and turn signal bulbs may be the standard automotive dual element type.

Bulbs with shattered glass must obviously be replaced, but it may be more difficult to identify other faulty bulbs. Extra new bulbs should be carried for emergency use and installing a new bulb is frequently more simple than other methods of checking. Corrosion, wiring failure, blown fuse and other problems can cause the bulb not to light. If changing the bulb does not solve the problem, a voltmeter, test light or other equipment may be necessary for checking.

Boat Supports

The entire weight of the boat is supported by the rollers or pads (bunks) while the boat is on the trailer. Improperly positioned or damaged roller or pad support can damage the boat while transporting or storing. Trailer manufacturers install a sufficient number of supports to handle the recommended boat weight, but it is important for the owner not to overload the trailer and to check for damage. Some trailers have supports which can be adjusted to support various boats. Positioning the support rollers or pads should be done by qualified personnel only. Return to the trailer dealer for assistance if you believe that supports are not correctly positioned.

Bunk supports should be recovered with appropriate padding material if original pad is torn, missing or damaged. Install new roller if damaged in any way. Each roller should be adjusted to hold proper amount of weight and to locate the boat in a nearly horizontal position. The real rollers or the aft most end of the bunk pads should support directly under the transom. Much of the boat's weight is attached to the transom, especially models with mounted outboard motors.

Tie-Downs

Use tie-downs to secure the boat's position on the trailer when the boat is being towed. If not tied down securely, the boat may move causing possible extensive damage to the hull or other parts. The boat may even slide completely off the trailer. Make sure that boat is resting properly on all supports before tightening any tie-downs.

⚠CAUTION

Tighten the tie-downs snugly but DO NOT attempt to force the boat against a trailer support by tightening a tie-down as hull damage may result.

WINTERIZATION AND STORAGE

GENERAL

You should always make special preparations for storing your boat and should never abandon it at the dock even if the storage is only for a short time. Extended storage and storage during winter or other severe weather should be thoroughly planned in advance and accomplished with the care that accurately reflects your concern. Specific storage procedures will vary greatly but some things to consider are as follows:

Where Should The Boat Be Located During Storage?

Small boats are easily and safely removed from the water, but the risk of damage to a large boat is so great that many are removed only during major refitting or repair. A larger number of boats fall into the middle range and the decision to remove the boat from the water is not simple. The decision to remove trailered boats from the water for storage is logical, but a trailer that is wrong for the boat, is damaged or is incorrectly adjusted may severely damage the boat. Many trailers don't provide support over enough area to adequately hold the boat for extended periods of storage without damage. Other procedures such as removal and storage by specially equipped and trained personnel or a special docking facility can also provide good alternative storage locations. The decision to remove the boat from the water and the storage location should be carefully considered. Check with other boat owners and local marinas to find what alternatives are most often considered by others with similar boats.

How Should The Boat Be Covered?

Properly fitted covers may be used to protect the boat from damage caused by sun, snow, rain and other potential sources of trouble. Improperly fitted, installed or supported covers may result in damage that you could avoid by exercising only slightly more care. Don't cover the boat too tightly. Allow proper circulation of air. Covers are available that are custom fitted to specific boat, motor and accessory combinations. Material is even available that permits air to pass through the cover, but not water. Cost varies, but is usually very reasonable.

Why Not Wait Until Next Spring To Fix It?

Normal use will result in wear and some damage but seldom does any of this interfere to the extent we must stop using the boat to repair it. This accumulated "slight" damage can amount to a significant amount during a boating season. Inspect all systems prior to storage and list **all** damage. Damage will seldom be **magically repaired** as you remove the boat from storage. The accumulation of wear that you "can take care of" may require much longer than you thought. It may be necessary to allow more time for repair or you may choose to get help. Repairs requiring professional service can often be scheduled during slack times for the repair shop at substantial savings. It can be really shocking to remove a boat from storage that was put away broken.

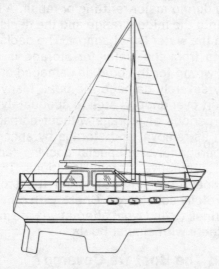

EXTERIOR

The complete exterior should be cleaned and waxed before covering and storing. Thorough cleaning and hand waxing not only protects the exterior but also provides an excellent opportunity to inspect the surface in detail. Repair or have qualified service personnel repair any damage to the hull. Even small cracks or seemingly slight damage should be inspected by a person qualified to determine the extent or potential for serious damage.

⚠WARNING

Any damage that affects the structural integrity of the boat should be repaired only by personnel with sufficient training and experience to accomplish the work. If qualified dealer or marina personnel believe that the successful repair will be impossible or very expensive, be extremely cautious about second opinions and bids for less costly repairs.

Inspect all seams carefully and repair or reseal any that may leak. Check seams especially around areas that were known to "leak a little." Water that leaks through the seams may run along some structural part of the boat and be first noticed a long distance away from the actual leaking seam. If water or water damage is noticed at any specific location in the boat, suspect that a seam is leaking.

The boat should be tipped up slightly and the drain plug should be removed during storage out of the water. Check often for accumulation of water and for leaves or other objects that could stop drain. Even if covered, moisture may accumulate inside boat if not permitted to drain. Be sure to reinstall drain plug before launching boat.

TRAILER

Special care should be exercised if the boat is stored on the trailer. Be sure that all of the rollers and/or pads are correctly positioned to properly support the weight of the boat. The boat can be easily damaged by storing it on a trailer with improperly positioned or damaged support rollers or pads. Refer to proper section for correctly adjusting trailer supports.

Trailer axle(s) should be raised and blocked to remove weight from the tires during extended storage. Wheels and tires may be removed from the trailer and stored in a cool, dry location if desired, but be sure that trailer is securely blocked to prevent falling. Covering the tires from the direct rays of the sun will reduce sidewall cracking, if stored out-of-doors.

INTERIOR

The interior should be cleaned and completely dried as storage begins. Sunlight, moisture, insects and rodents can damage boat interiors if not blocked out. Clean storage compartments and contents; then, carefully stow equipment. Discard any foodstuffs or similar material that may encourage entrance of pests. You may find it desirable to use insect or rodent repellent under certain conditions.

⚠WARNING

Follow manufacturer's instructions when using repellents. Do not use poisons, because of possible injury or death to people or pets and damage to environment. Dying rodents also tend to enter inaccessible areas where odor is impossible to remove.

Exposure to sunlight will fade and weaken carpeting, upholstery, curtains, etc. The gradual fading that occurs while the boat is in use will make it necessary to eventually repair or replace deteriorated material. However, sun damage may be slowed or even stopped by proper removal, cleaning and storage or perhaps, just blocking out the sun's rays by installing a cover. If curtains are removed, be sure to cover port holes to prevent sun damage to other interior surfaces.

⚠CAUTION

Tape will leave residue that is difficult to remove after a long storage. Never use.

Moisture even in the mild form of high humidity, can cause damage and odors. Many types of cloth and untreated wood are rotted by extended exposure to moisture, but mildew or other fungus can also permanently damage material that is otherwise impervious to water damage. Proper ventilation, air fresheners, mildew reducing agents and frequent cleaning will minimize odors and damage. Correctly fitted covers will effectively keep out moisture and sunlight and permit adequate air circulation.

BATTERIES

The boat should be winterized before removing the batteries, because winterizing some systems requires using the batteries.

Recharge batteries and add water as required. Disconnect cables and remove batteries, then store batteries in a cool, dry place. Check regularly and recharge as needed.

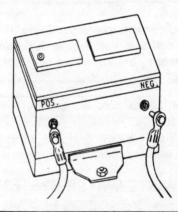

⚠CAUTION

DO NOT store batteries where they might be exposed to extreme heat or sparks.

POTABLE WATER SYSTEM

The fresh water system should be completely drained by opening all faucets and water line drain valves including those on the water heater and water storage tank. The following procedure is recommended: Open all faucets, valves and drains. Lock the toilet valve open (if of the mechanical seal type). This can be done by blocking the seal in the bottom of the bowl open with some object of the proper size being careful it does not fall through into the holding tank. If a water filter is installed, remove filter cartridge and drain lower portion of the housing. Turn water pump on and allow to run about two minutes, then turn pump switch off. Close all faucets, drains and valves, including toilet valve. Pour approximately six gallons of approved, nontoxic antifreeze into the fresh water storage tank. Turn water pump on and briefly open each faucet. Turn the faucets off when antifreeze flows out. Operate toilet until antifreeze is present in the bowl. Turn the water pump off. Leave all faucets closed during storage.

⚠CAUTION

Special nontoxic antifreeze is available at your marine or RV dealer. Do not use automotive type antifreeze in the fresh water system, because it is very poisonous.

Be sure to sanitize the potable water system as you remove the boat from storage. Refer to page 25 for sanitizing procedure. Check all components of the fresh water system for proper operation and for leaks.

WASTE WATER SYSTEM

Completely drain holding tanks of waste material. Flush sinks, shower and lavatory with solution of hot water, water softener and soap. Rinse well and allow solution to drain into holding tanks. Flush with clean hot water. Agitate water in holding tanks by rocking the RV, or drive vehicle a few miles. Drain holding tanks, flush with clean water and drain again. Fill traps and partially fill tanks with an antifreeze approved for use in plastic pipes. Normally two cups of antifreeze poured into each drain will fill the traps. Do not use antifreeze solutions with an alcohol base.

LP-GAS SYSTEM

Cover externally mounted LP-Gas regulator to keep moisture out of the vent. Close the LP-Gas service valves on tanks. Light a range burner to consume any gas remaining in the lines. When flame burns out, turn range burner off. LP-Gas tanks should have anhydrous methanol added by an LP supplier and tanks should be refilled to correct capacity.

When removing from storage use a soapy solution to check for LP-Gas leaks. Temperature variation and vibration will cause fittings to loosen and leak.

APPLIANCES

Refrigerator should be cleaned and the door propped open. Cover exterior panels and roof vents.

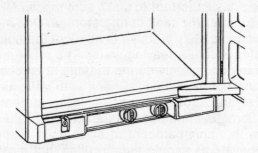

Furnace should be cleaned and exterior vents covered.

Range/oven should be cleaned, inside damper closed and range hood vent should be covered on the outside.

Air conditioner filters should be cleaned or renewed and installed and the shroud should be covered on the outside of the unit.

FUEL SYSTEM

The fuel system always requires special care and attention, but especially during storage. Fuels (gasoline and diesel) currently sold are much different than were available in earlier years and may require different handling procedures.

If possible, never use fuel for a marine engine that contains alcohol. Alcohol will absorb moisture and, when the water content exceeds 0.5% of the total amount of fuel and alcohol, the water and alcohol will separate from the gasoline. To put these quantities in amounts that are more understandable, 6 gallons of gasoline to which the refiner has blended one pint (10%) alcohol will separate if as little as a shot glass (1 fl. oz.) of water is added. The water may be from condensation, spray through a fill opening/vent or improper fuel handling by the marina before it is pumped into your boat's tank.

⚠CAUTION

Many additives sold as fuel stabilizers or dehydrators are primarily alcohol and should never be added to fuels already containing alcohol. Read the labels carefully.

It is especially important to make sure that water will not be permitted to enter the tank during storage. One method is to fill the tank completely so there is no room for moisture laden air that can condense, leaving water. The other method is to drain the tank completely during storage, then check and dry the tank just before refilling. Check with your fuel supplier, boat dealer and local marina for most current approved methods. Some manufacturers recommend coating inside of fuel tank with a small amount of oil to deter rusting in tank. Diesel fuel systems should remain filled, but most manufacturers recommend using an approved stabilizer mixed with the fuel in the tank. Filters should be serviced initially and water traps should be serviced regularly even while in storage.

ENGINE AND DRIVE SYSTEMS

Proper storage procedures can extend the life of powered equipment by preventing damage when not being used. Conversely, improper procedures, which is usually ignoring any preparation for storage, can accelerate deterioration and may directly cause damage.

Correct storage procedures will depend upon length of storage and the specific equipment. Refer to the manufacturer's recommended procedure for specific details. The following suggestions may be helpful for coordinating the storage with similar steps for removing the equipment from storage.

Service the cooling system to keep it from freezing. If engine has a closed cooling system, service with antifreeze to provide protection well below the anticipated lowest temperature. Do not attempt to drain all water from a closed cooling system to protect against freezing, because it is seldom possible to

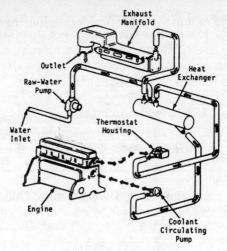

CLOSED COOLING SYSTEM

remove all water. A good quality antifreeze will also provide protection against rust and corrosion damage to the complete cooling system.

Open cooling systems that circulate water surrounding the boat to cool the outboard motor or the inboard mounted engine should be drained completely to prevent damage during storage. Damage caused by water remaining in the cooling

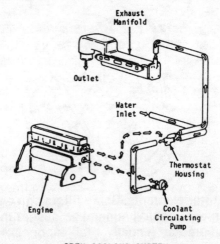

OPEN COOLING SYSTEM

system can be either freezing or corrosion. Expansion of ice resulting from low temperature can break metal (and other material) very easily. Corrosion, including rust, can be just as damaging, but is usually undetected until extensive erosion and blockage makes repair necessary.

Clean all cooling air passages and straighten, repair or renew any part which would interfere with normal flow of air.

Drain oil from all regularly serviced compartments such as engine crankcase, gearboxes, lower units, etc., while oil is warm. Refill with new approved oil to the level recommended by the manufacturer.

Clean and dry all exterior surfaces. Remove all accumulated dirt and repair any damaged surfaces. Paint exposed surfaces to prevent corrosion. Bare metal surfaces should be painted with an approved primer before painting with a color.

Inspect for worn or broken parts. Make necessary adjustments and repair all damage. Attach a description of wear and damage which is not fixed, then list all parts which have been ordered. Tighten all loose hardware.

Inspect and note condition of drive belts. If condition is questionable, a new belt should be installed, preferably when removing equipment from storage.

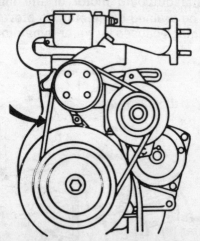

Install new filter elements. Some filters can be cleaned and serviced, but most should be installed new at this time.

Pour a small amount (usually 1 tablespoon) of oil into each cylinder of engine through hole for diesel engine injector or hole for spark plug on nondiesel engines. Crank engine with starter about 12 revolutions to distribute oil, then install spark plugs or injectors. Reconnect diesel fuel lines and spark plug wires.

Install protective caps at ends of all disconnected lines.

Seal exhaust and air intake openings. Special containers of moisture absorbing material are available which can be located inside the exhaust, before sealing.

Remove battery or batteries and store in cool, dry place. Do not permit battery to freeze and maintain fully charged, checking approximately every 30 days.

If necessary to store outside, an exposed motor and/or drive may be covered to prevent entrance of water, but make sure that cover is adequately ventilated. Sealing cover too tightly may cause condensation and accelerate major damage.

Observe the following when removing the engine or outboard motor and drive system from storage.

Remove all protective covers and check for moisture or obvious damage to the covering or covered equipment. Insects, birds, rodents or other pests may have used the protection of your boat and motor as winter shelter. Remove any moisture absorbing material that was installed when boat is entered into storage.

It is better to drain and safely discard old fuel from tanks and lines if the system has set more than three months, if boat has encountered a wide range of temperatures or if boat has been subjected to severe weather (rain, snow, etc.). Check drained fuel for evidence of water, rust or other foreign material and for unusual (rotten) smells. Fill the fuel tank with new approved type or mix of fuel before attempting to start. Check for leaks. Gaskets may dry up or carburetor needle valve may stick during storage. Repair any problems before attempting to start. Drain water traps and check condition of fuel filters. Bleed diesel fuel system following procedure outlined by manufacturer before attempting to start.

Check condition of battery or batteries and consider possible need for installing new battery. Be sure that correct type of battery is installed. All batteries are not alike so check with a qualified marine dealer if you have questions. Charge, then install the battery or batteries. Always remove the battery from the boat while charging. Clean battery posts and cables before attaching.

```
┌─────────────────────────────────────────────┐
│                 ⚠CAUTION                      │
├─────────────────────────────────────────────┤
│                                               │
│  Be sure that cables are attached to correct  │
│  terminals (posts) of battery. Many devices,  │
│  especially solid state components, will be   │
│  destroyed instantly if terminals are         │
│  reversed. Corroded battery terminals or      │
│  other conditions that result in excessively  │
│  high charging voltages can also damage       │
│  electrical components.                       │
│                                               │
└─────────────────────────────────────────────┘
```

Check condition of all filters (fuel, air, oil, water, etc.). Install a new filter, clean or service as required. Be sure that all protective coverings are removed and check for damage caused by insects, birds, rodents or other pests during storage.

Check condition and adjust tension of all drive belts as recommended by the manufacturer. Install new belts if condition is questionable.

Check for worn or broken parts and repair before returning to service. Coat all surfaces that are normally lubricated with approved type of oil or grease.

Check oil in all compartments such as the engine crankcase, gearboxes, lower unit, etc., for proper level. Evidence of too much oil may indicate water settled below the oil. Drain old oil if contamination is suspected or if time storage exceeds recommended time change interval. Fill to proper level with correct type of oil.

Fill engine closed cooling system, if so equipped, to correct level with approved coolant. Antifreeze solutions which improve summer cooling ability as well as providing rust and corrosion protection should be used. Check for leak if much fluid has leaked from closed cooling system during storage.

FIXES

These fixes include troubleshooting, because, after all, if you don't know what's broken, you don't know what to fix. The practical limit of repair will depend upon the skill and equipment of the person who is attempting to fix any given problem. This book is designed to supplement other published service manuals that cover specific repairs to specific components.

REPAIRING BOAT AND FITTINGS

CHECKING HULL DAMAGE

All of the damage may not be apparent to even trained personnel. Any damage that permits water to enter the boat is potentially dangerous and should be very carefully inspected. Cracks or holes in the hull or supporting frame may require extensive reinforcement to restore the integrity of the original construction. Be aware that the following conditions may exist regarding the hull damage:

1. Repair may require specially equipped and trained technicians.
2. Damage may be extensive to the point that repair is not practical.

⚠DANGER

It is always safer to have damage inspected by competent people who are experienced in repairing the specific type of construction. DON'T TAKE chances that may endanger the life or safety of the boat's crew or passengers.

HELPFUL HINT

A small hand saw with several different types of blades may be used to conveniently cut wood, fiberglass and even light metal if proper blade is available. Be careful and use a blade with close set teeth for the smoothest cut on finish wood, fiberglass, plastic and metal. Don't try to speed cut by forcing the blade into the material being cut.

HELPFUL HINT

Plumbers and electricians use a length of flexible steel or similar material to pull tubing, cables and wires through confined areas. This method is also convenient for fishing cables, wires, hoses, etc., through passages under the floor, behind a bulkhead or in other confined passages. Often a length of clothes hanger can be used for small lengths most common on boats.

FIXING ALUMINUM HULL

Three types of repair techniques are commonly used to repair aluminum hull damage: riveting, welding and epoxy compounds. Each type of repair has advantages that should be considered when repairing a damaged area.

Epoxy

Small damaged areas may be repaired using a two-part epoxy compound. The area should be relatively small, approximately ½ inch or less, and should not "work" or flex as the epoxy may lose its grip. The epoxy should be of thick consistency so it will not sag or run before hardening.

Before applying the epoxy, clean and abrade the area so bare metal is exposed. Read the manufacturer's instructions concerning application and apply a generous amount of epoxy. Spread the epoxy so it contacts bare metal around the damaged area for a better grip. If both sides of the damaged area are accessible, also apply epoxy to the inside of the hull for added strength. After hardening, it may be desirable to sand and paint the outer hull side, however, sanding may reduce the strength of the patch and if maximum strength is necessary, the patch should be left unsanded.

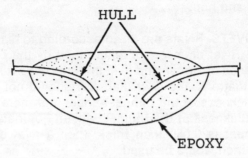

Epoxy may be applied to repair a small hole as described in text.

Riveting

The most common method of repairing aluminum hulls involves the use of rivets. Riveting is a simple, inexpensive means of fastening components together and requires a minimum of skill to perform. Riveting may be necessary to replace rivets which have loosened, broken off or fallen out. Riveting is also used to secure patches over damaged areas. Two types of rivets may be used to repair aluminum boat hulls:

1. Solid rivets
2. Pop rivets

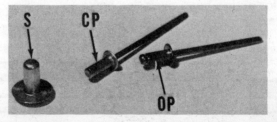

View of solid rivet (S), closed end pop rivet (CP) and open end pop rivet.

Standard rivets are one piece with a head and a solid shank. Pop rivets are two piece with a mandrel inside the rivet that forms the secondary head. Pop rivets are hollow after installation and should not be used in high stress locations or where maximum strength is required, such as structural members. Whether using standard or pop type rivets, only use aluminum rivets, otherwise, metal dissimilarity will cause corrosion between rivet and hull.

SOLID RIVETS. Rivets are sized according to diameter, grip and length. Rivet diameter is determined by the boat design engineer based on stress and rivet material. As a rule-of-thumb in repair situations, the rivet diameter should not be smaller than the thickness of the thinnest sheet, nor more than three times the thickness of the thinnest sheet. For instance, if the thinnest sheet is 0.050 inch thick, then a rivet diameter of 0.050-0.150 inch would be used.

Rivet grip is equivalent to the total metal thickness the rivet must clamp. Rivet length is the length of the rivet shank before installation. Rivet length of countersunk head rivets is measured from the top of the rivet head to the bottom of the shank. Rivet length on all other type rivets is just the shank length.

To determine correct rivet length, insert a rivet of the desired diameter and measure the standout from metal to end of rivet. Standout should be approximately 0.75 to 1.00 times the rivet diameter for countersunk rivets and 1.3 to 1.7 times rivet diameter for all other rivet types. As an example, an 1/8-inch diameter rivet should stand out 0.1625-0.2125 inch from the metal, so a rivet 5/16-inch (0.3125 inch) long would be selected if grip length is 1/8-inch (0.125 inch). A table of common rivet lengths for button head rivets is shown.

DIAMETER

		1/8 in.	5/32 in.	3/16 in.	1/4 in.
G	1/8 in.	5/16 in.	3/8 in.	3/8 in.	1/2 in.
R	1/4 in.	7/16 in.	1/2 in.	1/2 in.	5/8 in.
I	3/8 in.	9/16 in.	5/8 in.	5/8 in.	3/4 in.
P	1/2 in.	11/16 in.	3/4 in.	3/4 in.	7/8 in.

Suggested rivet length is listed in the yellow area at the intersection of the diameter and grip.

SELECTION. Rivets are available in a variety of head configurations. If an original rivet is being replaced, install a new rivet with the same head type as the old rivet. A boat may use more than one type of rivet head depending on rivet location, for instance, button head rivets may be used internally while countersunk head rivets may be used in the outer hull surface to reduce water turbulence. Button or truss head rivets are generally used when installing a repair patch.

Aluminum rivets are available in different alloys, and ideally, an aluminum rivet should be the same alloy as the aluminum it fastens. When performing small repairs, however, soft, type A rivets are used to ease installation.

BUTTON HEAD   PAN HEAD   TRUSS HEAD   COUNTERSUNK HEAD   FLAT HEAD

Drawing of various types of rivets. Note difference in measuring length (L) of countersunk and other type rivets.

INSTALLATION. Standard type rivets are installed by inserting the rivet, then deforming the shank end of the rivet to form a secondary head. As the secondary head is formed, the metal to be fastened will be clamped between the two rivet heads.

If not present, a straight, suitably-sized hole must be drilled to accept the previously selected rivet. The hole should be 0.003-0.008 inch greater in diameter than the rivet diameter. The accompanying table lists drill sizes for some common rivet diameters. Clearance between rivet shank and hole may be as much as 0.015 inch for rivet diameters ¼-inch or less, or 0.030 inch for larger rivet diameters, however, the use of these maximum clearances may result in ill-fitting rivets.

RIVET DIAMETER	DRILL SIZE	HOLE DIAMETER
0.125 in.	#30	0.1285 in.
0.156 in.	#21	0.159 in.
0.187 in.	#11	0.191 in.
0.250 in.	#F	0.257 in.
0.312 in.	#P	0.323 in.
0.375 in.	#W	0.386 in.

Refer to illustrations for procedure used to install an aluminum rivet. The head end of the rivet is "bucked" or held against the metal by a heavy object, usually a heavy metal block or hammer. The shank end of the rivet is then struck with the ball end of a light ball peen hammer until the shank is rounded over to form the secondary rivet head. Note that light, well-placed blows are preferred when forming the secondary head. Using excessive force may deform the underlying metal and produce a misshapened head.

The rivet secondary head is formed using the peen end of the ball peen hammer while "bucking" against the primary head. Several light blows are used to form the rounded secondary head.

View of rounded, properly formed, secondary head.

To prevent flattening the rivet head when bucking, a head set tool can be held against the rivet head. The head set tool may be purchased or made from scratch by machining a concave hole that will conform to the shape of the rivet head.

A head set similar to the one shown above may be used to prevent flattening the primary head during installation. Concave depression (C) is held against the rivet head.

To ensure watertightness, particularly if the rivet is regularly immersed, apply a pliable sealant to the rivet prior to installation. Check rivet watertightness after installation.

When more than one rivet is installed, rivets should be spaced so the distance between rivets is at least three times the diameter of the rivet. Rivets should not be installed closer than two times the rivet diameter from the edge of the metal.

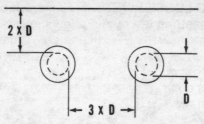

Diagram showing minimum desired distances between rivets and between rivet and edge of metal.

REMOVING RIVETS. Drilling is the correct procedure for removing a rivet. Rivets should not be chiseled off as the underlying metal will probably deform.

Before drilling, use a center punch guide dimple in center of rivet head. Select a drill bit slightly smaller in diameter than the rivet shank diameter and drill through the rivet. If the rivet diameter is not known, start with a small size drill bit then use progressively larger bits until most of the rivet is drilled away. If possible, do not drill into the metal hole. The rivet should now be sufficiently weakened so that the remainder can be driven free without damaging surrounding metal.

With the old rivet removed, inspect the metal hole for signs of wear and damage. If the hole will not satisfactorily accept the same diameter rivet as the old rivet, then the hole must be drilled to accept a larger rivet size.

Prior to drilling through a rivet, the rivet head must be dimpled with a center punch as shown to prevent the drill bit from wandering. Drill through the old rivet with drill bit the same size or slightly smaller than rivet diameter.

TIGHTENING LOOSE RIVETS. At times, a loose rivet may be tightened by resetting the rivet. Follow the same procedure as when installing a new rivet. Particular care must be used not to damage the surrounding metal so the rivet must be struck gently. If the rivet will not tighten, if the rivet is damaged or if the rivet hole is deformed, then the rivet must be removed and a new rivet installed.

POP RIVETS. Pop rivets are a two-piece type rivet that requires a special tool for installation. The rivet is tubular, with a mandrel that extends through the rivet. When the mandrel is pulled through the rivet, the mandrel head will upset the rivet and form the secondary head. The mandrel breaks off at the head when the rivet secondary head is forced against the metal being clamped.

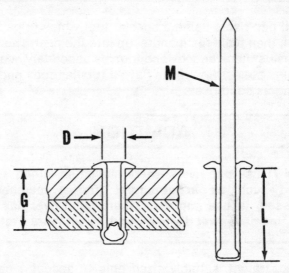

Drawing of pop rivet before and after installation. Note that mandrel (M) breaks off when forming rivet head.

Pop rivets are sized according to diameter, grip and length. Rivet grip is equivalent to the total metal thickness the rivet must clamp, **including back-up washers.** Rivet length is measured from the bottom of the rivet head to the end of the rivet, except for countersunk head rivets which are measured from the top of the rivet head to the end of the rivet.

Pop rivets are available in truss head and countersunk head configurations. Other designs may also be available but are seldom used for boat building or repair. Truss head rivets are generally used when installing a repair patch while countersunk rivets may be used in the outer hull surface to reduce water turbulence. Aluminum pop rivets may be equipped with either a steel or an aluminum mandrel.

⚠CAUTION

Use pop rivets with an aluminum mandrel only for repairing aluminum hulls. DO NOT use rivets that have steel mandrel or pop rivets with open end.

Install pop rivets using a special tool which grips the rivet mandrel, then pulls the mandrel up into the rivet. The mandrel head upsets the rivet body and forms a secondary head as the mandrel is pulled. Pop rivets have a tubular body and are not as strong as solid rivets.

⚠CAUTION

DO NOT use pop rivets where maximum strength is required such as in structural (frame) members. If necessary to use pop rivet where solid rivet has been used, increase rivet diameter and install more rivets.

Drill a straight, suitably sized hole to accept a new rivet. Rivet clearance in hole should be 0.003-0.006 inch for 3/32 inch diameter rivets, 0.004-0.008 inch for 1/8 and 5/32 inch diameter rivets, 0.005-0.009 inch for 3/16 inch diameter rivets, and 0.007-0.011 inch for ¼ inch diameter rivets. A #30 drill size is suggested for 1/8 inch diameter rivets; #21 for 5/32 inch diameter rivets; #11 drill bit for 3/16 inch diameter rivets.

To ensure watertightness, particularly if the rivet is regularly immersed, apply a pliable sealant to the rivet prior to installation. Check rivet watertightness after installation.

To install a pop rivet, proceed as follows: Open the rivet installation tool handles, then insert the rivet mandrel into the correct size tool hole. Note that most rivet tools have more than one diameter hole available and tool hole diameter should match the mandrel diameter.

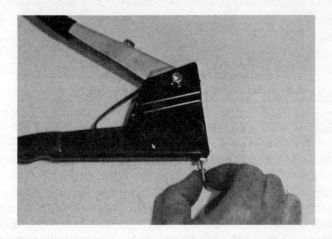

Insert rivet into rivet hole and install an aluminum back-up washer. Squeeze the rivet tool handles until the mandrel breaks off to form the rivet. Check the rivet to be sure it has tightened properly.

After mandrel breaks off, the secondary rivet head should be formed as shown.

REMOVING OLD POP RIVETS. Drilling is the correct procedure for removing a rivet. Rivets should not be chiseled off as the underlying metal will probably deform. Select a drill bit slightly smaller in diameter than the rivet shank diameter and drill through the rivet. If the rivet diameter is not known, start with a small size drill bit then use progressively larger bits until most of the rivet is drilled away. If possible, do not drill into the metal. The rivet should not be sufficiently weakened so that the remainder can be driven free without damaging surrounding metal.

With the oil rivet removed, inspect the metal hole for signs of wear and damage. If the hole will not satisfactorily accept the same diameter rivet as the old rivet, then the hole must be drilled to accept a larger rivet size.

Welding

Special equipment and skill is necessary for welding aluminum. Boats of welded construction may require repair by welding. Boats of nonwelded construction may also be successfully repaired by welding. Welding should be performed only in a shop suitably equipped by personnel experienced in welding aluminum.

If information is desired concerning welding equipment, procedures and safety requirements for aluminum, contact the American Welding Society at the following address:

American Welding Society
2501 N.W. 7th Street
Miami, Florida 33125

Removing Dents

Aluminum alloys for marine use are malleable and usually stretch before tearing. Some dents may be removed by simply pressing on the bulge of the dent to force the hull back to its original shape. If dent will not press out, then careful use of a rubber mallet or composition hammer and a piece of wood, referred to as a buck, may be used. With the buck positioned on concave side of dent, slowly work the dent with light blows starting from the outer edge proceeding in a circular motion toward the center. It may be necessary to drill a small hole in the center of large dents to allow for metal displacement. Once dent has been removed, hull should be checked for stress cracks and hole (if drilled) filled with a suitable epoxy. It may be preferred to repair hole by installing a rivet with sealer around its shank or by welding.

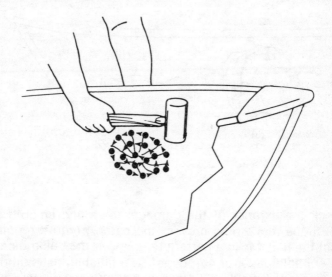

Dents that will not respond to cold working may be removed by careful application of heat. Because aluminum does not change in color when heated as do ferrous metals, this procedure must be done with extreme caution.

Slight irregularities in the hull surface may exist after dent removal and may be smoothed out using a suitable fairing compound.

Crack Repair

Damage to a boat hull resulting in a tear or crack may be repaired with the installation of a riveted or welded patch. The following information covers riveted patch installation.

Patch material should be of the same alloy originally used in the hull. If the original aluminum alloy is not available, a substitute alloy of a higher temper number or thicker gage should be selected.

Before patching, drill a 3/16 inch crack arrestor hole at the end of each crack or at the base of each tear. This should stop further spreading of an existing crack. Work the damaged area back to its original shape using the same procedures outlined in the Dent Repair section. Check carefully for other stress cracks and drill additional holes where required.

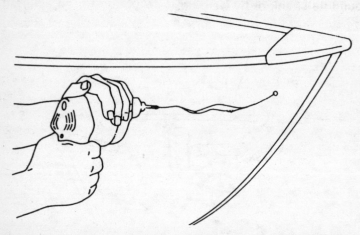

Check the exterior of the damaged area and smooth any obstructions that would prevent the patch from fitting close against the hull. Make a pattern template of the desired patch using suitable paper or cardboard. The finished patch should extend one inch past any crack or hole. Oval or rectangular shapes are preferred, but all corners should be rounded. Check template for fit and make sure that it is sufficiently large to cover the damaged area with enough room for rivets around the edge.

If cardboard template is difficult to fit, the patch will also require shaping to follow the contour of the hull. Be sure patch has enough metal to permit shaping.

NOTE

Template can be enlarged slightly using heavy masking tape around edge.

Press the template against hull and mark around circumference with a crayon to help ensure proper alignment of patch. Transfer the shape of the template to suitable aluminum repair sheet, then cut the patch to the desired size and shape. Clean the edge of patch with a file, sand paper or scraper to remove any sharp edges.

Shape the patch to follow the contour of the hull closely and be careful that patch is located according to the position indicated by the crayon mark.

Difficult shapes may require hammering patch around a buck or wooden form. Concave shape can be accomplished by pounding center of patch, stretching the metal in the middle. Be careful to match the shape to the hull.

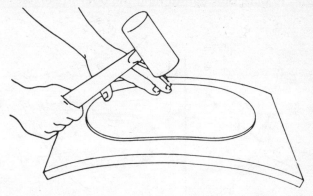

Mark, then centerpunch the rivet locations around the edge of patch. Refer to the preceding section for information on rivet selection, spacing and installation procedures. Hold the patch in place over the damaged area, then drill a hole of the proper size for the rivets through the patch and the hull. Insert a tight fitting bolt through the holes, then install and tighten a nut to hold the metal together. Drill similar holes at center punched locations through patch and hull, installing bolts and nuts temporarily to maintain alignment.

NOTE

The two pieces should be firmly, but temporarily attached as each hole is drilled, to ensure correct alignment of all holes. Bolt and nuts of the proper size can be used successfully, but other methods can also be used. Special spring loaded locating clips and a plier type of installing/removing tool is available from suppliers specializing in aircraft sheet metal tools. Some repair shops use sheet metal screws to temporarily hold the patch in place.

After all holes are drilled, remove the nuts and bolts, then lift patch off. Remove metal burrs from around the drilled holes, make sure patch and hull are cleaned, then apply sealer around riveted area of patch. Reinstall patch and secure in place with rivets as described in the preceding section. Wipe off excess sealer from around patch, then allow sufficient time for sealer to cure before returning the boat to service.

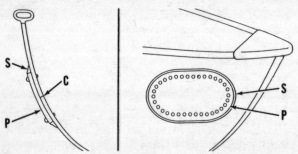

Views of external patch (P) installation to cover crack (C). Apply sealer (S) as outlined in text.

Fairing Imperfections

Dents ⅛ inch or less in depth and slight irregularities in the hull surface may be removed using a suitable fairing compound. Nonmetallic fillers intended for marine use should be used. Automotive type fillers and fillers containing metal are not recommended.

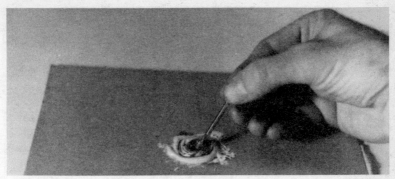

Thoroughly clean the damaged area and remove all paint and grease. Paint may be removed with 50 to 80 grit sandpaper and finish sanded with 180 grit paper. Read and follow the manufacturer's mixing instructions carefully, then using a flexible plastic applicator, apply filler to damaged area. Apply the filler with smooth downward and sideways strokes ensuring all air bubbles are removed and that filler extends a sufficient distance around damaged area to allow filler to blend into original hull surface. Make certain filler has cured before sanding.

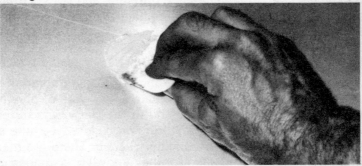

Best sanding results can be obtained using a dual-action orbital sander. Circular sanders are not recommended. Use an 80 grit paper then start sanding in a back and forth motion until all high spots are removed. Finish sand the area with 180 grit paper by first using a back and forth motion to feather the filler edge so there are no discernible places where the filler contacts the aluminum hull. After feathering the filler edges, use a circular motion over the entire area following the hull contour. Complete the repair by using a back and forth motion for approximately five or six strokes.

Paint the repaired area and inspect the area for imperfections. Reapply filler if required to further smooth surface.

FIXING FIBERGLASS

Fiberglass is actually a porous type material, the gel coat (outer color coat) is what forms the smooth exterior finish on the hull. As the gel coat ages and begins to wear away, the pores within the coating will become more prominent. Nature's natural elements, such as sunlight and salt water, attack the gel coat surface causing it to fade and soften. Stains soak deeper into the enlarged pores and are more difficult to remove.

Restoring Gel Coat

To restore the gel coat appearance on badly deteriorated, oxidized or marked surfaces, the damaged layers of gel coat must be removed to get to the fresh gel coat surface underneath. Before starting restoring procedures, be sure exterior surface has been thoroughly cleaned. There are many different methods being used for the removal of damaged gel coat. Following are some of those methods.

The slowest but safest method of gel coat removal is by using rubbing compound. Using a suitable buffer and rubbing compound, rub out entire surface of hull. Selection of proper rubbing compound grit to start with is dependent upon the condition of the exterior surface. On badly deteriorated surfaces, a more abrasive compound should be used first, whereas for less severely damaged finishes a milder compound should be used. Move to a finer grit compound each time until a finishing compound is used. After completely rubbing out entire exterior surface, rewash surface as outlined earlier, then apply wax coating to surface as required. Using clean buffing pads or suitable equivalents, polish wax coating to a high luster.

A slightly faster method is by starting with a fine grit wet sandpaper (between 320 and 400 grit). Caution should be taken when using sandpaper not to penetrate gel coat. After removing damaged gel coat, complete gel coat restoration by using a suitable buffer and rubbing compound as previously outlined. Rewash surface and wax as required.

Using acid solutions, such as muriatic acid or phosphoric acid, to etch the damaged gel coat away is a fairly quick but hazardous method. Without the experience or safety knowledge of using acid solutions, this operation should be left to the professional. To use the acid, wipe it on the damaged surface and then rinse it off quickly to etch away the damaged gel coat.

⚠CAUTION

Do not leave acid solution on surface for any length of time as gel coat will be severely damaged and have to be renewed.

After removing damaged gel coat, complete gel coat restoration by using a suitable buffer and rubbing compound as previously outlined. Rewash surface and wax as required.

⚠WARNING

Injury may result from acid contacting skin. Use protective clothing to prevent contact with skin and eyes. Make sure that neutralizing solution, water (for flushing affected area) and proper medication are quickly available before beginning to use any acid.

Major restoration of gel coat is usually only possible **once** during coating life without renewal of coating since gel coat is a fairly thin coating. For this reason, do not remove any more coating than is necessary to prolong life of gel coat.

HELPFUL HINT

Always use a clean container or scoop to transfer any catalyst activated repair compound. Contamination of unused material may cause hardening of all or part of the material.

Fiberglass Repair

A repaired fiberglass hull should have strength equal to that of the original construction, if properly done. The quality of the finished repair, is however, affected by:

1. Surface preparation
2. Cleanliness
3. Complete and correct mixing of repair products
4. Proper lamination of reinforcement

Proper repair of structural damage is critical to the performance of the boat and to the safety of the crew and passengers. Improper repairs may mask serious problems and can cause injury or death. Repairs involving the structural integrity of the boat should only be accomplished by experienced and qualified people, who are equipped and trained to properly repair fiberglass boat hulls.

Cosmetic damage can be repaired easily and includes cracking, surface scratches and gouges. This type of damage affects the appearance and not the structural soundness of the boat. Structural damage may occur if certain types of surface damage is not repaired.

Use a suitable cleaning solvent to thoroughly clean the damaged area, then inspect the area closely to be sure that no structural damage has occurred. Cut a "V" groove along the scratch using a sanding sleeve or burr driven by a power drill or rotary tool. Use 100-220 grit sandpaper to remove rough edges and feather surface back beyond scratch.

Wipe sanding residue from surface, then use compressed air to clean the scratch groove.

⚠CAUTION

During surface preparation, do not touch repair area with fingers or hand as body oils could be absorbed into unprotected surface. Gloves may be worn to prevent contamination.

Prepare a blend of gel coat and Cab-O-Sil, then apply material in a forceful manner to minimize chance of air entrapment. Overlap scratch or hole approximately 1/16-inch with gel coat.

Spray PVA on repaired area or cover with a strip of cellophane and squeegee down. **Repair area must be completely covered for gel coat to cure.**

Allow gel coat to completely cure, a minimum of 1-2 hours is required. After gel coat has completely cured, remove cellophane strip or wash PVA from surface with water.

Sand surface using 220-600 grit wet sandpaper until joining lines between repair area and hull surface are smooth and unnoticeable. Wipe residue from surface, then thoroughly rinse off repaired area with fresh clean water. Rub surface out by using a suitable buffer and a fine grade rubbing compound. Be careful when using buffer around corners and edges, gel coat can be easily cut through. Wash entire surface removing all residue, then apply wax coating as required.

PAINTING

Testing Old Paint

ADHESION TEST. Before repainting, old paint should be tested for adherence and compatibility. Using a single-edge razor blade, sharp knife or other suitable cutting tool, make 10 parallel cuts approximately 1/16-inch apart through the paint. Then make 10 parallel cuts perpendicular to the previous cuts so a crosshatch pattern is formed as shown. Apply ¾ inch wide number 600 Scotch cellophane tape to cut area; be sure tape is pressed firmly against paint. Pull tape off sharply in a parallel direction to surface. If paint is not removed with tape, then paint adhesion is satisfactory and area may be repainted without removing old paint. However, if old paint is removed with tape, then the old paint should be removed before applying new paint.

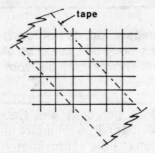

Procedure for performing paint adherence test.

PAINT COMPATIBILITY. If old paint adhesion is satisfactory, then compatibility between old and new paint must be determined. Paint a small test patch over the old paint in an inconspicuous area. Check for blistering, lifting or softening of test area paint. If no problems are encountered, then new paint should be compatible with old paint. To check adhesion of new paint to old paint, perform the adhesion test outlined in the previous paragraph.

Paint Removal

If old paint is cracked, blistered or did not pass the adherence test, then paint must be removed from entire hull. If antifouling paint is to be renewed, then only old antifouling paint should be removed if underneath gel coat surface is in good condition.

NOTE

Some antifouling paints are applied directly to new fiberglass hulls without a priming coat. Some paint manufacturers recommend using a priming coat to ensure good sealing of pores in hull. Be sure to follow paint manufacturer's recommendations.

Two methods may be used to remove old paint from a fiberglass boat hull: mechanical paint removal or chemical paint removal.

PAINT STRIPPING. Chemical paint removal is commonly termed "stripping" and uses a chemical agent to etch away surface coating. Be sure to use only a recommended solution and to follow directions outlined by manufacturer.

⚠WARNING

Injury may result from chemical strippers contacting skin. Wear acid-resistant gloves, clothing and face protection at all times when working with any caustic solution. Make sure that neutralizing solution, water (for flushing affected area) and proper medication are available quickly before beginning.

After stripping solution has set for manufacturer's recommended time period and stripping procedures have been followed, flush surface with clean fresh water to remove residue.

MECHANICAL REMOVAL. Mechanical paint removal is accomplished by abrasive blasting or sanding. The surface must be cleaned prior to proceeding so dirt, oil or other particles are not worked into the surface. Abrasive blasting (commonly called sand blasting) should be done at a low air pressure setting to prevent damaging hull. When sanding, start with a medium grit (100-120) sandpaper then use a fine grit (280-320) sandpaper. Sand surface until all oil paint is removed.

Thoroughly wipe hull clean with a suitable cleaner. Do not allow solution to evaporate on surface and change cloths frequently so as not to reposition residue, but to wipe surface clean.

SURFACE PREPARATION

Amount of preparation on surface to be painted is dependent upon the condition of the surface. A hull that is not damaged and has passed the adherence and compatibility tests as previously outlined will require only minimal preparation. Remove wax coating if present, then lightly sand surface with a medium grit sandpaper to remove surface gloss. The following precautions should be followed when sanding hull surface:

Excessive sanding may cause pores in gel coat to become open or pitted.

⚠CAUTION

When sanding an antifouling coating, always wear a respirator mask to prevent inhaling toxic chemicals contained in coating. It is also recommended that a long sleeve shirt and cap be worn. Be sure to shower thoroughly to remove toxic paint particles from skin. Wash before eating or placing any other object around the mouth that could cause toxicants to be ingested.

Surface should be cleaned after sanding. Some sandpapers are treated with a solution to prevent clogging while sanding, but a residue is left after sanding. After sanding use a suitable cleaning solvent and thoroughly wipe off hull surface.

If hull surface is damaged, repair before proceeding with surface preparation.

Applying paint

Make sure surface preparation has been done correctly and completely before proceeding with application of paint. A beautiful paint job will fail in a very short time if the surface preparation underneath was not done correctly.

Always keep painting area as clean as possible to prevent new paint from becoming contaminated. Ideal curing temperature for paint, unless stipulated differently by manufacturer, is 75°F. Temperatures between 60°F and 80°F are acceptable working temperatures. Paint will cure slower at a cooler temperature than at a warmer temperature. In most cases the reducer or thinner used in mixing the paint to a thinner consistency is available in different drying speeds. During hot weather a slower drying reducer or thinner should be used to retard the curing time and vice-versa when painting in cooler weather.

Do not expose painted surface to any type of moisture during early stages of curing. Excessive surface moisture may cause paint to flatten and lose gloss. Use caution when painting on hot days; exposure to direct sunlight rays may cause paint to blister.

Paints are designed to be applied by either spraying, rolling or brushing. Some manufacturer's do not recommend rolling paint on, because there is a tendency for roller nap to leave air pockets in paint. A recommended practice is to roll paint on, then brush paint in vertical strokes. When brushing, use two brushes and change brushes frequently. Clean and soak brush not being used in a suitable reducer or thinner. When changing brushes, allow brush that was soaking to thoroughly dry before using. Changing brushes frequently is to prevent paint from curing in base of brush.

If using spraying equipment, always make sure air lines are free of water and oil particles.

⚠WARNING

When preparing surface for painting, wearing gloves is recommended to prevent body oils from being absorbed into unprotected surface.

Boats that are removed from the water frequently and boats that are used in fresh water do not require antifouling paint coating. Boats that remain in salt water for extended lengths of time (or full time) may benefit from an application of antifouling paint.

After determining boat usage, select a paint system from a paint manufacturer and use only the products in that paint manufacturer's system; do not mix products. Manufacturers formulate paints to be compatible with their own paints and mixing paints of different manufacturers may produce undesirable results.

The number of coats and the thickness of coats is dependent upon many items, such as, the painting procedure you are using, the type of products you are using and the condition of the surface you are painting. The manufacturer's painting procedures should be followed where stipulated, however, the following recommendations should be helpful.

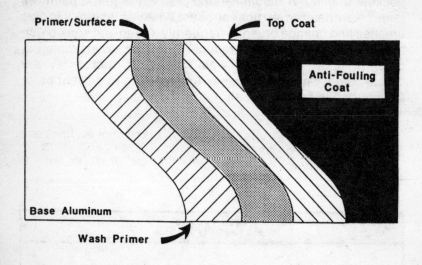

FRESH-WATER HULL. Of primary importance regardless of the brand of paint used, is the cleanliness of the hull surface. Clean and wash hull as previously outlined and allow surface to dry completely.

If the original paint is to be retained, perform paint adherence and compatibility tests as previously outlined. Sand the surface to remove loose paint, surface gloss and to roughen surface for better paint adherence. Be careful not to sand excessively and cause pores in gel coat to enlarge.

Primer paints are designed to serve several different purposes such as: a filler for surface imperfections, a sealer for fiberglass pores and an undercoat where paint cannot be applied directly to fiberglass. Some primers must be sanded in between coats, while sanding is not recommended on some primers. Primer paint must be compatible with the topcoats. Be sure to follow manufacturer's recommended application procedures closely. Procedures may vary from manufacturer to manufacturer and from one type of primer paint to the other.

After the primer has dried and, if necessary, sanded, the topcoats are applied per manufacturer's recommendations. Several types of topcoat paints are available and type of boat usage should be considered before a selection is made. Generally, the tougher, more durable topcoats are more expensive so cost must be matched with how and where the craft is used.

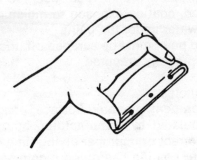

Be sure to use the type of paint suitable for the application. Do not attempt to spray paint that is intended to be applied by brush. Apply paint in the manufacturer's recommended number of coats and in the film thickness recommended. It is always better to apply two or three thin coats, than to apply one thick coat which runs and/or sags. Follow paint manufacturer's instructions. Some surfaces may be recoated if paint has not cured for longer than 36 hours. After 36 hours, surface must be lightly sanded with a fine grit (280-320) sandpaper before recoating.

If metallic type paint is being used, topcoat must be sprayed on surface to attain uniform depth and maximum gloss. Mix paint thoroughly as described by the paint manufacturer, then apply the paint in the number of thin coats suggested. Too heavy a coat will cause metallic sag, runs and uneven distribution. After applying color coat, a clear coat should be applied following suggested application procedure.

Following is a troubleshooting list that may be used in diagnosing paint failures.

Problem: Low gloss, wrinkling or poor drying
Cause: Paint applied too late in day, applied when ambient temperature is too cool, or applied too thick.
Solution: After coating has cured recommended length of time, sand to a smooth surface, then apply another coat under proper working conditions.

Problem: Peeling, bubbling or poor adherence
Cause: Improperly prepared surface, too thin of coat applied, coating exposed to moisture before cured or water under the paint.
Solution: Bad paint must be scraped off, then surface must be properly prepared.

Problem: Pinholes
Cause: Improperly prepared surface, paint not mixed as stipulated by manufacturer, spraying technique incorrect or improper drying time between coats.
Solution: After coating has cured recommended length of time, sand to a smooth surface, then apply another coat following manufacturer's recommended procedures.

Problem: Orange peel or rough uneven surface
Cause: Surface too hot, spraying technique incorrect, improper spray gun pressure, paint viscosity is too high or solution for reducing paint is wrong.
Solution: After coating has cured recommended length of time, sand to a smooth surface, then apply another coat following manufacturer's recommended mixing and application procedures.

Problem:	Fish eyes or small craters
Cause:	Inadequate surface preparation, wax or silicone on surface, contaminated painting equipment or excessive fish eye preventative contained in old finish.
Solution:	Clean contaminated equipment as needed. After coating has cured recommended length of time, sand to a smooth surface, then apply another coat following manufacturer's recommended procedures.
Problem:	Paint sag
Cause:	Paint viscosity is too thin or paint applied too heavily.
Solution:	Follow manufacturer's mixing procedures, then apply paint in a thinner coat.

SALT-WATER HULL. Boat hulls which are constantly immersed in salt water or brackish water require protection from the formation of marine organisms. Protection is provided by an antifouling paint which is toxic to marine organisms thereby preventing their formation on the hull. The paint consists primarily of a binder and the toxic, antifouling agent. The binder carries the toxicant as well as other paint ingredients and adheres the paint to the hull surface. In most types of antifouling paint, the toxicant particles gradually leach through the paint to the surface to provide antifouling protection until the toxicant is spent. In co-polymer type antifouling paint, the toxicant particles are exposed as the paint is worn away.

Most paints are available in a soft, medium-hard or hard film group. The softer and cheaper paints are used on slow moving boats in low fouling water conditions, while the harder and more expensive paints are used on fast moving boats where hard film along with excellent antifouling properties are needed.

Boat usage and painting skills must be considered when selecting an antifouling paint system. Rosin based antifouling paint is "soft" and not as long lasting or durable as the plastic based (epoxy, acrylic, urethane, etc.) paints. However, the plastic based paints may require painting techniques that should be performed by a professional painter with proper equipment.

Most antifouling paints in use contain copper or tin compounds as their toxic agent.

⚠WARNING

When sanding or spraying antifouling paints, always be sure to wear a respirator mask to prevent inhaling toxic chemicals contained in coating. It is recommended that a long sleeve shirt and cap be worn. Be sure to shower thoroughly to remove toxic paint particles from skin. Wash before eating or placing any other object around the mouth that could cause toxicants to be ingested.

Cleanliness is of primary importance, regardless of the brand of paint used. Clean and wash the hull thoroughly, then allow the surface to dry completely.

If the original paint is not completely removed, perform paint adherence and compatibility tests as previously described. Sand the surface to remove loose paint and gloss from the surface, then rewash hull surface and allow to dry completely.

Some paints are not designed to be applied directly to fiberglass coating. A suitable undercoat must be applied between antifouling paint and fiberglass surface. Antifouling paint may be applied by roller, brush or spraying. **Be Sure** to use application procedure that is designed for that specific type of paint. Apply paint using paint manufacturer's recommended number and thickness of coats. Stir paint well before applying, then stir occasionally while using to ensure equal distribution of toxicant particles.

Some boats must be immersed much sooner than others after antifouling paint is applied, toxicant particles may start to decompose if left exposed to the air.

If a co-polymer antifouling paint was applied, **DO NOT** use a pressure hose when washing surface. The high water pressure will cause paint coating to be washed off hull surface.

There are many factors which influence the longevity of antifouling paints. Listed below are items which could cause premature failure of antifouling paint.

1. Water level low
2. Fresh water from heavy rains
3. Water temperature too high or too low
4. Water salinity too low
5. Acid or alkaline content too high
6. Paint coat too thin
7. Heavy slime conditions
8. Electricity charge loose in area
9. Immersion time incorrect
10. Poor surface preparation
11. Porous fiberglass

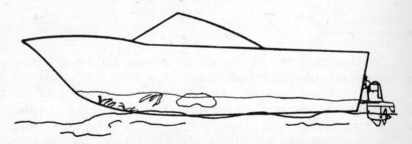

Low water level may cause boat bottom to lie in mud. The contaminates within the mud may neutralize the paint and the mud coating will plug the paint surface stopping toxicant particles from leaching to the surface. The scraping of boat bottom may cause paint to be removed and leave bottom unprotected in this area.

Fresh water washed in from heavy rains will bring in silt and food. The silt will coat the boat bottom and the food will nourish the marine organisms. The influx of fresh water will also lower the salinity of the water, thus slowing down the leaching of the toxicant particles and temporarily affecting the antifouling action against marine organisms.

Water temperatures that are above or below average will alter toxicant release rate. Warmer water will cause toxicant particles to be released more quickly. Cool water will retard fouling and when water temperature falls below 50°F fouling all but stops.

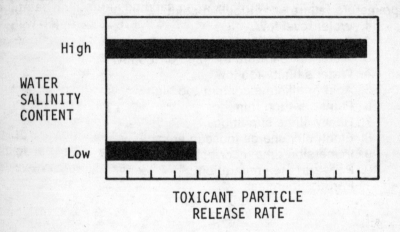

TOXICANT PARTICLE
RELEASE RATE

Waters that are low in salinity content will have a slow release rate of toxicant particles.

Waters that have been infected with acid or alkaline will affect the leaching rate of toxicant. Too much alkaline in water will stop the leaching of toxicant particles and in some cases may completely plug if off. If acid content is too high, the toxicant particles will be depleted quickly leaving antifouling coat ineffective.

Paint should be applied using manufacturer's recommended number of coats and thickness of coat. Too little paint applied may cause toxicant particles to be released before year is out and antifouling coat left ineffective.

Heavy amounts of slime accumulated on boat bottom will slow release rate of toxicant and could cause it to be stopped completely. Slime can also hold on to the silt from the water, and silt will start fouling boat bottom.

Electrical components installed and improperly grounded will release uncontrolled electricity in the area. The electricity may neutralize the antifouling paint causing fouling to occur.

Be sure to wait the recommended time before immersion. If boat is launched before paint has dried, the paint may remain pasty, blister or partially wash away. If boat is left out too long, the coating may dry too hard and cause toxicant leaching rate to be retarded or plugged off. In some cases, light sanding may reopen coating to allow toxicant to leach through. Be sure to observe safety precautions when sanding antifouling paint.

Surface preparation cannot be taken lightly, a paint job will fail in a very short time if the surface preparation was not done correctly. Always follow manufacturer's recommended procedures for preparing the surface for paint.

Porous fiberglass that absorbs water will blister and cause paint to pop off. Boats that are hauled at the end of the year may experience this problem.

Due to some of the conditions that affect the longevity of antifouling paint, the extent of fouling will vary from year to year. An antifouling coating that fails one year due to heavy

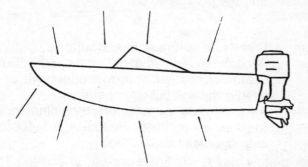

fouling conditions may last the following year if fouling conditions are lower. The more attention paid to the bottom of the boat, the longer the antifouling coating will last. If boat bottom is kept clean of slime, dirt or fouling, the toxicant particles will be allowed to leach from the paint at a steady and correct rate.

Following is a troubleshooting list that may be used in diagnosing antifouling paint failures.

Problem: Blistering
Causes: Porous gel coat or poor surface preparation.
Solution: Antifouling coat must be completely removed by sanding or using suitable chemical removers. If gel coat is found to be bad, gel coat must be patched following recommended procedures or removed completely. Following manufacturer's preparation and application procedures install a suitable undercoat, then apply antifouling paint as stipulated by manufacturer.

Problem: Premature failure
Causes: Recommended number of coats and thickness of coats not applied, boat was immersed too soon or too late, paint not suitable for area or paint not stirred thoroughly.
Solution: Always follow manufacturer's recommended procedures as outlined. Antifouling coat must be renewed after performing complete and correct surface preparation.

Problem: Premature failure of motor outdrive paint
Causes: Recommended number of coats and thickness of coats not applied, incorrect undercoat or primer used or heavy fouling conditions.
Solution: Always follow manufacturer's recommended procedures as outlined. Periodically inspect lower unit and clean as needed.

Problem: Peeling from underwater metal parts
Causes: Preparation of parts poor or incorrect primer or undercoat used.
Solution: Parts must be thoroughly cleaned, then painting procedures as stipulated by manufacturer must be followed.

ENGINE AND DRIVE REPAIR
REMOVE AND INSTALL PROPELLER

The propeller may be splined onto the drive shaft or a pin may be used to transfer rotation of the drive shaft to the propeller.

⚠️WARNING

Be sure ignition is "OFF" and gear selector is in "NEUTRAL" when servicing propeller, otherwise, accidental starting can occur if propeller shaft is rotated.

Splined Type

Propellers which have a splined hub also have a rubber cushion ring that surrounds the hub and absorbs shock should the propeller strike an obstruction. This type propeller is held on the propeller shaft by a nut.

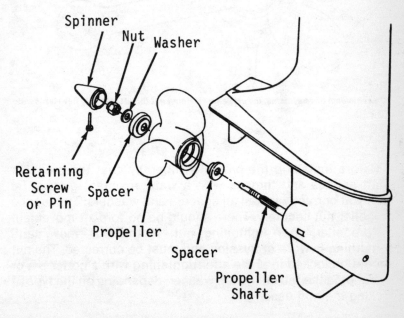

Spinner
Nut
Washer
Retaining Screw or Pin
Spacer
Propeller
Spacer
Propeller Shaft

If the spinner has two flat sides, it probably is threaded to the shaft. Remove the retaining screw, clip or pin, then remove the spinner. Unscrew the nut then slide the propeller off the shaft to remove the propeller. Don't lose any washers or spacers which may also be found on the shaft.

Occasionally, the nut may be rusty or extremely tight. Apply a lubricating solvent to shaft threads to loosen rust. If needed, a block of wood may be positioned between the propeller and the antiventilation plate to prevent propeller rotation while unscrewing the nut.

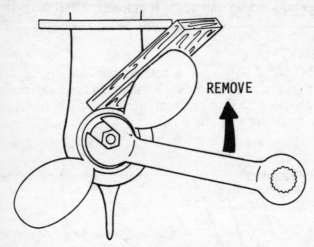

REMOVE

On some dual drive systems, the propeller retaining nut for left side may have left-hand threads.

Before installing the propeller, liberally coat the propeller shaft splines and threads with a water-resistant grease. Be sure you correctly install all spacers and washers. Tighten the propeller nut securely. There should be no fore-aft movement of propeller after tightening nut; if there is movement, something is worn or missing and must be corrected. The nut should be locked in place after tightening with a cotter pin or by bending the tab on the tab washer, depending on the type of locking method used.

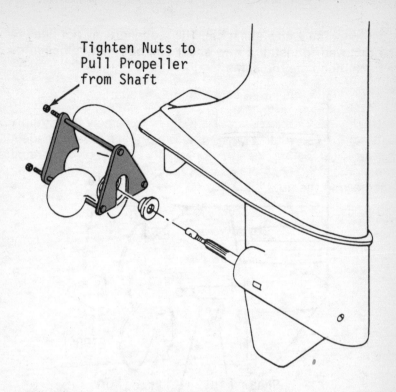

Tighten Nuts to
Pull Propeller
from Shaft

HELPFUL HINT

A puller can be purchased or fabricated as shown to help remove props that are stuck on the shaft. The metal must be thick and strong enough to resist bending. Tighten the screws evenly to prevent damage to end of shaft.

Shear Pin Type

The drive pin is designed to break (shear), if the propeller strikes an underwater obstruction, protecting other drive system parts from damage. The shear pin is made of a specific type of metal and is a specific size for each drive system. Several spare shear pins and spinner retaining cotter pins should be carried at all times for emergency replacement. It is also important that all operators recognize the evidence of a broken shear pin, know where extra pins are stored and be able to install a new shear pin. The propeller may not need to be removed to install a new shear pin, but many procedures and cautions are the same.

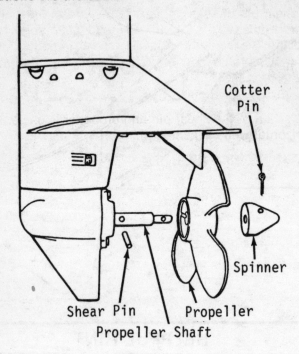

Remove the cotter pin or retaining clip from the spinner, then carefully withdraw the spinner.

⚠CAUTION

Be prepared to catch the shear pin, as the spinner is withdrawn. The shear pin may fall from the holes in propeller and propeller shaft as the spinner is removed.

Remove shear pin from propeller and shaft, then remove the propeller.

⚠CAUTION

The shear pin of some models is located at front of propeller. If holes and shear pin are not visible at rear after removing the spinner, carefully slide propeller toward rear and be prepared to catch the drive (shear) pin from in front of propeller.

Installation of the shear pin and propeller is easier if holes are horizontal while assembling.

⚠CAUTION

Install ONLY shear pins specified for use by the manufacturer of the drive or outboard motor. Substitute only in an emergency, then install correct pin as soon as possible. Extensive damage can result if pin is too strong. Normal operation may break pin if material is too soft.

NOTE

Spare shear pins should always be carried aboard, but in an emergency, the broken parts can sometimes be assembled as shown.

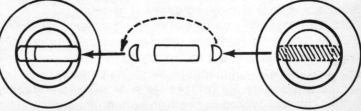

The resulting pin has only ½ the shear strength of a new pin, but may permit powering into port. Other combinations, such as two of the longer center sections are also possible for some models.

ENGINE TROUBLE-SHOOTING

Repair is divided into three areas: Recognition that a problem exists; Locating the source of the problem; and Correcting the trouble.

Delay can be costly. Problems should be noticed quickly so that diagnosis and repair can begin. Delay may cause further damage and injury.

Internal combustion engines really require very little to start and to run.

1. A combustible mixture of fuel and air must be in the proper place and must be compressed enough to encourage ignition easily.
2. Nondiesel engines require an ignition source, timed and positioned to provide desired ignition of the combustible mixture. Diesel engines must inject the fuel into the flow of air that is compressed enough to provide ignition of the fuel.
3. The burned (expanded) fuel and air must be removed from the cylinder.
4. Uninterrupted engine operation depends upon the smooth continuation of the previous processes.

Occasionally, serious mechanical trouble will develop, but usually problems are very minor. Some may not even happen if you properly clean, lubricate and maintain your boat, its motor, controls and drive. Don't attempt service that greatly exceeds your skill. Service manuals are available to assist you with some repair, but only trained technicians should be allowed to accomplish certain tasks. Consult appropriate service manuals and your authorized dealer if in doubt.

The two most likely causes of engine problems are the ignition and fuel systems. Some engines have carburetor adjustment screws that are just too handy to overlook, even for experienced service personnel. Most carburetors now use specific sized metering orifices (jets) or mixture adjustment needles that are locked in position so that indiscriminate adjustment is impossible or at least much more difficult.

Although not always at fault, the quality of the fuel should be checked if the engine suddenly begins to run poorly or is more difficult to start. Fuel (any type or mixture) that is old should be discarded.

NOTE

Observe local ordinances when discarding anything. Petroleum products including most fuels and lubricants constitute a fire hazard as well as an environmental polutant. Check local authorities for suggested disposal methods.

Fuels can be unsuitable for operation because of evaporation, contamination, biological growth or some other reasons. Don't take a chance with old or new fuel that may be bad. A small amount of water, varnish, etc., can result in a service nightmare.

After making sure that tank is filled with sufficient amount of good quality fuel, check the condition of the spark plugs. A damaged spark plug may not be visually obvious and some new plugs may be worse than those removed. Be sure that new plugs are of the correct type, including heat range, and that gap between electrodes is set to distance recommended by the engine manufacturer.

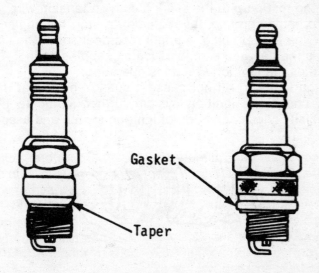

Gasket

Taper

Will Not Start Or Is Hard To Start

All engines need fuel to start and run. Check to be sure that the fuel tank is filled with the proper type of fuel. Water or other incorrect fluid in the tank can prevent the engine from running and may cause extensive damage. Water doesn't mix with gasoline or diesel fuel and will appear as different colored areas floating in the fuel. Clean water is clear (lighter in color), but water can be colored by rust and be darker. A large amount of water in the fuel tank can cover the bottom of the tank uniformly and may be difficult to identify.

Check to be sure that controls are properly positioned. Interlocks may prevent starting unless the safety switches are correctly set. It is also important to have the choke or other starting enrichment properly set before attempting to start.

Spark ignition engines need a correctly timed spark and a proper mixture of fuel and air in the combustion chamber to operate. Other problems can prevent the engine from starting or to be hard to start, but the most probable causes are lack of fuel or lack of spark. Remove the spark plug and check condition after attempting to start. The spark plug should have the odor of gasoline and may be damp appearing, but should not be fouled or obviously damaged.

A test plug can be purchased from many suppliers of ignition service tools. The gap should be approximately ⅛-inch. Attach the test plug to the spark plug high tension wire, attach clip to engine ground, then attempt to start the engine while observing the test plug. A bright electrical spark should jump across the gap and should cause a snapping sound. A spark indicates the ignition system is operating.

If the ignition will not cause a spark regularly at the test plug, check the ignition system further to locate trouble. Especially check condition of ignition switch and associated wiring.

If the ignition is operating satisfactorily, the problem is probably in the fuel system. The problem could be caused by other failure, but remember to check the simplest items first.

On diesel (compression ignition) engines, the engine must compress the air sufficiently, then fuel must be sprayed into the compressed air. Failure or difficulty in starting is related to the compression or injection.

If possible, check exhaust from diesel engine while attempting to start. A light colored vapor indicates some injection and failure or difficulty in starting is probably caused by a failure to compress the fuel enough. Low cranking speed can also make starting difficult.

If compression appears normal, loosen a high pressure fuel line at one of the injection nozzles and attempt to start engine. If fuel spurts from the loosened connection at regular intervals while attempting to start, fuel is attempting to be injected.

If fuel does not flow from the loosened connection, begin at the fuel tank and follow the path of fuel through the filters and transfer pump to the injection pump until the cause of the difficulty is located. Some causes of the fuel not flowing are air in the lines, plugged fuel filters and incorrectly adjusted fuel shut-off controls. Be sure that the correct line is loosened for this check.

If fuel flows from the loosened injection line, remove injection nozzle from cylinder head, then attach nozzle to a suitable tester. If nozzle tester is not available, nozzle can be reconnected to injection line of engine with nozzle spray directed outside cylinder. Again attempt to start the engine or operate tester and observe nozzle spray pattern. A finely atomized spray should be injected regularly from the nozzle. The desired shape of the spray cones will depend upon the design of the nozzle.

⚠DANGER

The fuel is released from the nozzle with sufficient force to penetrate the skin. Do not risk injury by permitting the high pressure spray to contact any part of the body.

If fuel sprays from the nozzle, check compression pressure and inspect for mechanical damage such as burned valve, leaking head gasket, etc. If compression is satisfactory, check injection timing.

If fuel spurts from the loosened high pressure fuel line connection, but does not spray from the exposed nozzle, service the fuel injection nozzle. A ragged spray which is not properly atomized can cause difficulty in starting.

On all models, the starter must turn the engine fast enough to start. Damaged starter, low battery charge or any other problem that slows down the starting speed, may prevent the engine from starting.

Be sure that safety interlocks are operating properly and will permit starting.

Engine Starts, Then Stops

This complaint is usually due to fuel starvation, but may be caused by a faulty ignition system. Recommended trouble-shooting procedure is as follows:

Remove and inspect fuel tank cap; on many models of outboard motors, the fuel tank is vented through breather in fuel tank cap so that air can enter the tank as fuel is used. If engine stops after running several minutes, a clogged breather should be suspected. It is usually possible to let the engine run with fuel tank cap removed and if this permits engine to run without stopping, clean or renew the cap.

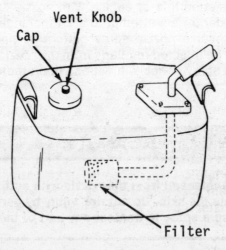

Vent Knob

Cap

Filter

⚠CAUTION

Be sure to observe safety precautions before attempting to run engine without fuel tank cap in place.

If there is any danger of fuel being spilled on engine or spark entering open tank, **do not** attempt to run engine without fuel tank cap in place. If in doubt, try a new cap.

A separate vent line is used for built-in tanks. Check these systems similarly if a clogged vent is suspected cause of fuel starvation.

If clogged vent is eliminated as cause of trouble, a partially clogged fuel filter or fuel line should be suspected. Remove and clean fuel tank and line and if so equipped, clean fuel shut-off valve and/or fuel tank filter. On some engines, a screen or felt type fuel filter is located in the carburetor fuel inlet; refer to specific engine repair manuals for details.

NOTE

Biological growth can occur in the fuel tanks which will affect engine operation. This growth often becomes noticeable after removing from storage, but will continue to grow if not treated. Products are available that will stop further growth, but old contaminated fuel must be drained and tank must be cleaned.

After cleaning fuel tank, line, filters, etc., if trouble is still encountered, a sticking or faulty carburetor inlet needle valve, float or diaphragm may be cause of trouble. A trained servicing dealer can remove, disassemble and clean carburetor using appropriate service data and specifications.

If fuel system is eliminated as cause of trouble, check ignition coil on tester if such equipment is available. If not, check for ignition spark immediately after engine stops. Renew coil, condenser and breaker points if no spark is noted. Also, on four-stroke cycle engines, check for engine compression immediately after engine stops; trouble may be caused by sticking intake or exhaust valve or cam followers (tappets). If no or little compression is noted immediately after engine stops, consult a servicing dealer.

Engine Overheats

The engine can be seriously damaged by too much heat. High engine temperature can be a result of the cooling system not removing enough heat or the engine creating too much heat.

Heat is removed from air cooled engines by radiating heat to the surrounding air. If engine overheats, check for bent or missing cooling air housings. Do not operate an air cooled engine without all shields and blower housing in place. Also, check for dirt or debris accumulated on or between cooling fins. Broken fins can cause localized hot spots that may increase overall temperature.

Liquid cooled engines may use either a closed, recirculating type cooling system (as normally used on automobiles) or an open circuit system. Most boat motors use an open circuit cooling system, which draws a small amount of water from around the boat, circulates the water through the engine to abort heat, then expells this heated water back to the surrounding water. Any cooling system failure that slows or stops circulation of cooling fluid will prevent cooling.

On most outboard motors, liquid coolant flow is held at a relatively constant level regardless of engine speed by the design of the coolant pump. Most use a rubber impeller type pump located in the lower motor leg, just above the lower unit drive gears. The rubber impeller is lubricated by the water its pumping while operating normally and will be quickly damaged if operated dry. A thermostat is often used to assist in maintaining an efficient operating temperature by recirculating coolant water until desired temperature is reached. The thermostat may fail, but the pump impeller is more easily damaged. Age, heat, abrasive (sand) or other problems can cause the impeller to deteriorate. Parts of the old impeller can lodge in the coolant passages and cause engine to overheat, even after installing a new impeller.

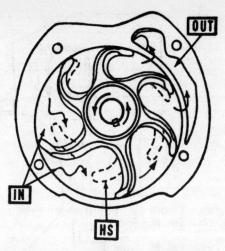

Schematic drawing of a typical rubber impeller type water pump which maintains an approximately equal volume of coolant flow at most operating speeds. Water is drawn into pump (IN) as area between vanes increases and is forced into power head (OUT) as area decreases. At high speeds (HS) the blades remain curved and pump operates mostly by centrifugal action.

The water used to cool the engine of almost all inboard engines and outboard motors is passed into the exhaust system to cool and quiet the exhaust. If the exhaust exits through the lower motor leg or outdrive unit, a small hole above the water line is provided to visually check for coolant water flow. Water should be seen exiting the telltale hole with engine idling.

The accessory drive belt usually drives the coolant pump of inboard engines. Failure to pump water (or other coolant) may be caused by a broken or loose drive belt. If belt slips, check the coolant pump for freedom of rotation. Install a new water pump if difficult to turn with belt removed from drive pulley. Damaged bearing or seal in water pump can cause pump to lock.

All gasoline powered engines can overheat if operated with the fuel mixture too lean, or with ignition timing occurring at the wrong time. It is also possible to overload the engine, causing it to overheat, by installing the incorrect propeller.

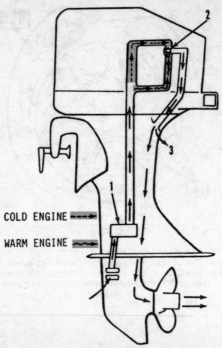

Drawing of bypass type cooling system thermostat operation used in some motors. When power head temperature is below normal the thermostat (2) closes coolant outlet through power head and opens the bypass outlet. Coolant flow then follows course shown by broken arrows (Blue). As operating temperature is reached, thermostat opens coolant passages through power head and closes bypass. The coolant then flows through power head as shown by wavy arrow (Red). The coolant pump is in lower unit as shown by (1). At idle, water is discharged from small hole (3) of most outboard motors.

Electrical System Problems

The electrical system consists of parts and connecting wiring to provide engine starting, ignition spark, battery charging, operation monitoring, communication and other functions. Logical trouble-shooting will usually center on the system that is most directly affected. It may, however, be necessary to expand the search to include related systems. An example could be failure to start caused by a dead battery resulting from a failure of the alternator to charge the battery.

IGNITION CONDITION CHECK. If the engine will not start and the ignition system is suspected, make the following checks to find the cause of the trouble.

A test plug simliar to the one shown can be attached to a spark plug wire and grounded while attempting to start the engine. Observe the gap at the test plug. Be sure that ignition switch is set to "ON", "START", "RUN" or similar position. A bright spark should jump across the gap at the test plug with an audible snap at regular intervals. A regular spark at the test plug usually indicates that the ignition system is OK; however, the ignition timing may need to be adjusted. Failure to produce a spark indicates ignition system problems requiring additional checks.

If ignition at the test plug is satisfactory, remove and inspect the spark plug or plugs. If the plugs are fouled or otherwise questionable, install new spark plugs of the correct type with recommended gap, then attempt to start.

If spark does not occur or is irregular at the test plug, check condition of breaker points or ignition timer and the ignition coil.

BREAKER POINTS AND CONDENSER. Remove cover, and using a small screwdriver, separate and inspect breaker points.

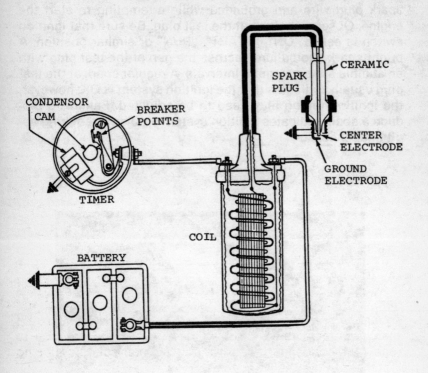

CONDENSOR
CAM
BREAKER POINTS
CERAMIC
SPARK PLUG
CENTER ELECTRODE
GROUND ELECTRODE
TIMER
COIL
BATTERY

If burned or deeply pitted, install new breaker points and condenser. If point contacts are clean to grayish in color and are only slightly pitted, proceed as follows: Disconnect condenser and ignition coil lead wires from breaker point terminal and connect a test light and battery between terminal and engine ground as shown. Light should go on when points are closed and should go out when points are open. If light fails to go out when points are open, breaker arm insulation is defective and new breaker points must be installed. If light does not go on when points are closed, clean or renew the breaker points. In some instances, new breaker point contact surfaces may have an oily or wax coating or have foreign material between the surfaces so that proper contact is prevented. Check ignition timing and breaker point gap as outlined in an appropriate engine repair manual.

Connect test light and battery between condenser lead and engine ground; if light goes on, condenser is shorted out and should be renewed. Capacity of condenser can be checked if test instrument is available. It is usually good practice to renew the condenser whenever new breaker points are being installed if tester is not available.

VOLTAGE, WIRING AND SWITCH CHECK. If no spark, or a weak yellow-orange spark occurred when checking system as outlined in preceding paragraph, proceed with following checks:

Test battery condition with hydrometer or voltmeter. If check indicates a dead cell, renew the battery; recharge battery if a discharged condition is indicated.

NOTE

On models with electric starter or starter-generator unit, battery can be assumed in satisfactory condition if the starter cranks the engine freely with spark plugs installed.

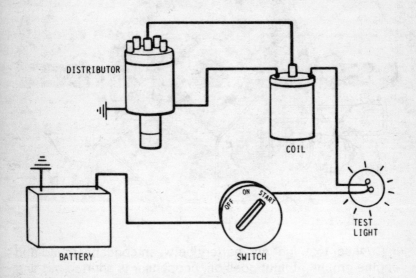

DISTRIBUTOR

COIL

BATTERY

SWITCH
OFF ON START

TEST
LIGHT

If battery checks OK, but starter unit will not turn engine, a faulty starter unit is indicated and ignition trouble may be caused by excessive current draw of such a unit. If battery and starting unit, if so equipped, are in satisfactory condition, proceed as follows:

Remove battery lead wire from ignition coil and connect a test light of same voltage as the battery between the disconnected lead wire and engine ground. Light should go on when ignition switch is in "on" position and go off when switch is in "off" position. If not check for safety interlock switches in wiring. Some interlock switches may require certain conditions (such as starting only in NEUTRAL) before current is supplied to ignition. It may be necessary to check wiring schematic for specific unit to locate all of the interlock switches. Also, be sure to isolate and check condition of the ignition switch.

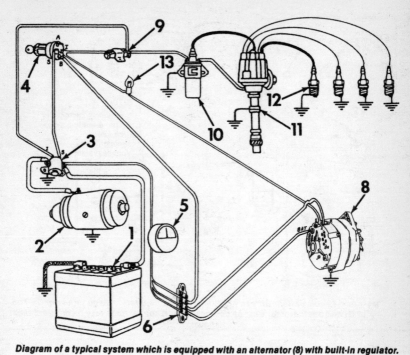

Diagram of a typical system which is equipped with an alternator (8) with built-in regulator.

The terminals of many electrical components are marked; however, a universal code is not used. Some of the more common marks are identified as follows:

A or ARM. Armature on generator or voltage regulator.

A or ACC. Accessory terminal of switch.

B or BAT. Battery (ungrounded lead).

F. or FLD. Field.

G. or GEN. Generator insulated output terminal.

GND. Ground connection for unit.

I. or IGN. Ignition.

L. Charge indicator light circuit.

R. Regulator on alternator or voltage regulator. May provide ½ of normal system voltage to operate certain accessories.

R. Starter solenoid or relay circuit used to bypass ignition system resistor when starting.

S, ST or START. Starter activated terminal of switch, starter or solenoid or relay.

S or SW. Main control switch terminal of voltage regulator.

STA. Stator connection on alternator.

1. Charge indicator light terminal on alternator.

2. Terminal which should be connected to battery ungrounded lead to controlling internal regulator of alternator.

Consult responsible, competent service shop experienced in electrical repair of the equipment for help with specific problems.

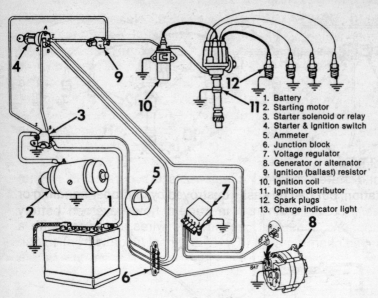

1. Battery
2. Starting motor
3. Starter solenoid or relay
4. Starter & ignition switch
5. Ammeter
6. Junction block
7. Voltage regulator
8. Generator or alternator
9. Ignition (ballast) resistor
10. Ignition coil
11. Ignition distributor
12. Spark plugs
13. Charge indicator light

Diagram of a 12 volt system with an alternator (8) and separate voltage regulator (7). The regulator (7) and alternator (8) must be compatible and connections may be different than shown.

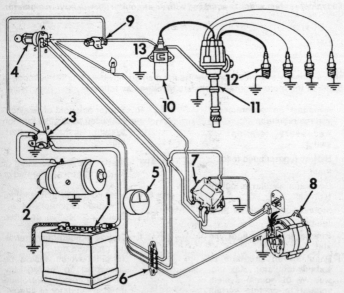

The charge indicator light (13) operates on the difference in voltage between the two connections. When voltage at battery and charge voltage at terminal "L" of regulator are the same, charge indicator bulb will not light.

SOLID STATE IGNITION CHECKS. Nearly all ignition systems which use solid state electrical components are capable of generating more emf than conventional systems. It is therefore easier to bridge large air gaps, some of which may not occur at the spark plug of a properly running engine. The high tension circuit, including spark plug wires, distributor cap, etc., must be in excellent condition to prevent electrical discharge at an improper location. Cracks in the spark plug wires may cause engine to misfire, but can also result in personal injury.

Solid state electrical components are durable in normal operation, but can be easily destroyed by improper handling or abuse. Forcing a change in current flow (reversed battery connections, loose or disconnected wires, operating with a damaged charging system, etc.) and heat (usually from soldering) are the most common causes of solid state component failure.

Often failure to obtain adequate spark from an ignition system is caused by loose or corroded connections which must make good contact, or a short circuit to ground at locations which should be insulated from ground. Either of these conditions can result in damage that requires new components, but sometimes correcting the problem is all that is necessary to restore spark.

Because of the differences in solid state ignition design and construction, it is impractical to outline general service procedures. It is important to refer to the applicable service manual before trouble-shooting or repairing any of these systems. Some cautions to be observed are as follows:

1. Use ONLY approved procedures when testing to prevent injury or damage.

2. DO NOT reverse battery terminals.

3. DO NOT disconnect battery while engine is running or attempt to start engine with battery missing from system.

4. DO NOT disconnect **any** wires while engine is running or ignition switch is on.

5. Install only recommended spark plugs, tachometer, accessories and replacement parts.

6. Always disconnect battery ground before completing any work which could result in short circuit.

Setting Breaker Point Gap

Changes in the breaker point gap affect ignition timing and ignition strength, so the gap should be carefully and accurately adjusted to the specifications suggested by the manufacturer. The breaker points of some engine models can be inspected and adjusted through a hole in the flywheel or after removing the distributor cap, but for other models, it may be necessary to remove the flywheel. Check an appropriate service manual for correct procedure necessary for a specific engine model. Install a new breaker point set if old parts are questionable.

Adjust breaker point gap as follows unless specific service instructions apply. On some engines, it is necessary to adjust the breaker gap to obtain correct ignition timing. First, turn engine so that points are closed to be sure that the contact surfaces are in alignment and seat squarely. Then, turn engine so that breaker point **opening is maximum.** Use a clean greaseless feeler gage to measure the gap and be sure points are not pitted. New breaker contact point set should be install-

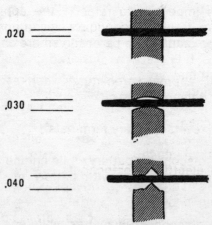

Irregularities on point surface can give false gap reading. In the three examples a 0.020 inch feeler gage is used; actual gap varies from 0.020 to 0.040 inch.

ed before proceeding if old breaker points are pitted. Contact surfaces must seat squarely and properly align when points are closed.

Different procedures are necessary to change the breaker contact gap. A common procedure is to loosen retaining screw (R). Insert the blade of a screwdriver in notches (N), then change the gap by turning screwdriver. Be sure to recheck gap after tightening screw (R). It is important to set gap between points to the clearance specified by the manufacturer in the engine repair manual.

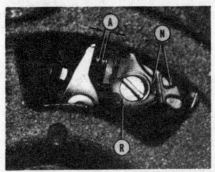

Some ignition systems may have opening in flywheel for adjusting breaker points.

A. Point gap
N. Adjusting notches
R. Retaining screw

Service Notes For Solid State Ignitions

Nearly all ignition systems which use solid state electrical components are capable of generating more emf than conventional systems. It is therefore easier to bridge large air gaps, some of which may not occur at the spark plug of a running engine. The high tension circuit, including spark plug wires, distributor cap, etc., must be in excellent condition to prevent electrical discharge at an improper location. Cracks in the spark plug wires may cause engine to misfire, but can also result in personal injury.

Solid state electrical components are durable in normal operation, but can be easily destroyed by improper handling or abuse. Forcing a change in current flow (reversed battery connections, loose or disconnected wires, operating with a damaged charging system, etc.) and heat (usually from solder-

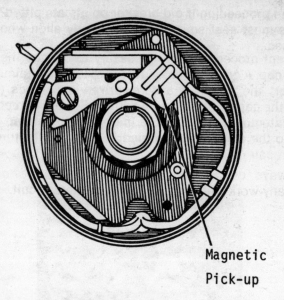

Magnetic
Pick-up

ing) are the most common causes of solid state component failure.

Often failure to obtain adequate spark from an ignition system is caused by loose or corroded connections which must make good contact, or a short circuit to ground locations which should be insulated from ground. Either of these conditions can result in damage that requires new components, but sometimes correcting the problem is all that is necessary to restore spark.

Because of the differences in solid state ignition design and construction, it is impractical to outline general service procedures. It is important to refer to the applicable service manual before trouble-shooting or repairing any of these systems. Some cautions to be observed are as follows:

1. Use ONLY approved procedures when testing to prevent injury or damage.

2. DO NOT reverse battery terminals.

3. DO NOT disconnect battery while engine is running or attempt to start engine with battery missing from system.

4. DO NOT disconnect **any** wires while engine is running or ignition switch is on.

5. Install only recommended spark plugs, tachometer, accessories and replacement parts.

6. Always disconnect battery ground before completing any work which could result in short circuit.

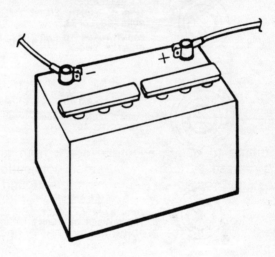

CARBURETOR REPAIR AND ADJUSTMENT

Carburetor repair and adjustment should only be attempted by properly trained service personnel with correct test and adjustment equipment. Some engines, especially early models, have easily accessible mixture adjustment needles (screws) that are too often twisted at the first sign of any change (or imagined change) in engine performance. Most later engines use fixed orifices (jets) or sealed adjustment screws to thwart unnecessary changes.

Standard carburetor adjustment is usually correct for lower altitudes, but may be too rich (too much fuel) for operation at higher altitudes. Be extremely careful about operating engines at low altitudes, if carburetor has been adjusted for mountain or high plains use, because the resulting lean mixture may cause overheating and engine damage. Check with authorized servicing dealer if carburetor repairs or adjustments are necessary. Service manuals are available covering the specific engine model which will assist you in servicing fuel filtering systems.

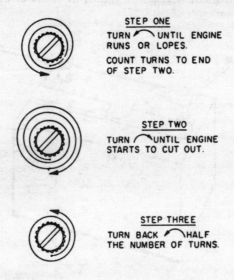

STEP ONE

TURN ⌒ UNTIL ENGINE RUNS OR LOPES.

COUNT TURNS TO END OF STEP TWO.

STEP TWO

TURN ⌒ UNTIL ENGINE STARTS TO CUT OUT.

STEP THREE

TURN BACK ⌒ HALF THE NUMBER OF TURNS.

Turning the adjustment needles may adjust the air or the fuel permitted to pass the metered orifice. If fuel is metered, turning the needles clockwise will lean the mixture and counterclockwise rotation will enrich the mixture. Idle mixture must be adjusted at idle speed and higher speed mixture at the appropriate higher speeds. All mixture adjustments should be adjusted with engine operating at applicable load. Mixtures that are correct with no load or only minimum load will probably be far too lean during normal operation. The lean mixture may cause overheating and severe engine damage.

New "HOW-TO" Maintenance & Tune-up Manuals

**OUTBOARD MOTOR
MAINTENANCE & TUNE-UP
MANUAL
FIRST EDITION, VOLUME ONE
Cat. No. OMM1-1**

Here's everything the boat "do-it-yourselfer" needs to maintain and tune-up his outboard motor. "Written for the average owner"—not mechanic (Intertec's Outboard Motor Service Manuals provide teardown and reassembly information for the professional mechanic.)

Easy-to-use two-column format, large illustrations, and easy-to-follow instructions are featured in this manual. This manual covers virtually all manufacturers of outboard motors below 30 horsepower.

8"x11", softbound   264 pages
ISBN 0-87288-224-1   List Price: **$12.95**

**OUTBOARD MOTOR
MAINTENANCE & TUNE-UP
MANUAL
FIRST EDITION, VOLUME TWO
Cat. No. OMM2-1**

This manual covers virtually all manufacturers of outboard motors with 30 horsepower and above for the owner interested in maintaining his own outboard motor.

8"x11", softbound   264 pages
ISBN 0-87288-225-X   List Price: **$12.95**

Plus, owner's manual

**BOAT
OWNER'S MANUAL
FIRST EDITION
Cat. No. BOM-1**

Here's a comprehensive guide for first-time boat owners (with information which even veteran boat owners will appreciate).

Safety...rules of the road...boat operation...storage...emergency information...boat identification...legal requirements...the list goes on and on with answers provided to virtually all questions posed by boat owners. A section on trailers provides information on towing, hitches, safety, brakes, tires, lighting and other topics.

This is a book which takes the guesswork out of boat ownership—a book which should be in every boat glove compartment.

5½"x8", softbound   160 pages
ISBN 0-87288-184-9   List Price: $4.95

Available from

MARINE SERVICE MANUALS

OUTBOARD MOTOR SERVICE MANUAL
NINTH EDITION, VOLUME ONE
Cat. No. OS1-9

Here's everything you need to service most major brands of outboard motors.

A comprehensive fundamentals section provides detailed tips on periodic servicing, troubleshooting, general maintenance and general repairs.

The special service section contains specifications and step-by-step servicing procedures on hundreds of models with less than 30 hp. Virtually every major brand is included. In most cases, 1969 through 1982 model years are covered.

8"x11", softbound   344 pages
ISBN 0-87288-188-1   List Price: $11.95

NINTH EDITION, VOLUME TWO
Cat. No. OS2-9

Provides the same detailed fundamentals on periodic servicing, troubleshooting, general maintenance and general repairs as volume 1.

The special service section focuses on specifications and servicing procedures for motors with 30 hp and above.

8"x11", softbound   250 pages
ISBN 0-87288-189-X   List Price: $11.95

OUTBOARD MOTOR FLAT RATE MANUAL
EIGHTH EDITION
Cat. No. OF-8
8"x11", softbound   52 pages
ISBN 0-87288-012-5   List Price: **$10.95**

OLD OUTBOARD MOTOR SERVICE MANUAL
FIRST EDITION, VOLUME ONE
Cat. No. OOS-1

By popular request...a perfect complement to the Outboard Motor Service Manual. Here's a manual that covers older makes and models of outboard motors under 30 hp produced prior to 1969. Many pages are reproduced from out-of-print Technical Publications manuals. A fundamentals section covering design as well as service fundamentals leads the mechanic through all types of repair and maintenance procedures.

8"x11", softbound   264 pages
ISBN 0-87288-186-5   List Price: $14.95

FIRST EDITION, VOLUME TWO
Cat. No. OOS-2

Provides detailed fundamentals on periodic servicing, troubleshooting, general maintenance and repairs on motors 30 hp and above produced prior to 1969.

8"x11", softbound   240 pages
ISBN 0-87288-187-3   List Price: $14.95

INBOARD ENGINES & DRIVES SERVICE MANUAL
SECOND EDITION, VOLUME ONE
Cat. No. IBS1-2

Everything you need to know about servicing, troubleshooting and repairing the most popular makes and models of gasoline and diesel inboard engines used on power boats and sailboats.

8"x11", softbound   160 pages
ISBN 0-87288-024-0   List Price: $10.95

SECOND EDITION, VOLUME TWO
Cat. No IBS2-2

Provides the same detailed information on servicing, troubleshooting and repairing as volume 1.

8"x11", softbound   216 pages
ISBN 0-87288-050-8   List Price: $10.95

Available from

INTERTEC
PUBLISHING CORPORATION